The Savoury Chocolate Cookbook

ISBN
978-1-989647-48-6

A Byrd Press Publication
Toronto
www.byrdpress.com
publisher@byrdpress.com

Art Direction by GrucType
Cover Design Dina Walker

dedicated to necessity, the origin of all inventions

but, inspired by Sat Bains, Enrique Olvera, Richard Sandoval, Grant Achatz, Irma Rombauer, Michael Field, Waverly Root and every cocoa farmer around the globe

also by Andrew West

The Instant Chef: American Classics

Bark & Bite: Culinary Canine Creations for a Happy,
Healthy Hound

The Savoury Chocolate Cookbook

by Andrew West

Purpose, Use and Formatting Notes

Crafted to go beyond the ordinary, this book intertwines interpretations of traditional cocoa and chocolate recipes with avant-garde creations. It invites readers into a realm where each recipe serves as a brushstroke on a canvas of art—a moment for reflection, a catalyst for shared experiences, and an opportunity for culinary experimentation. More than a mere compilation of instructions, it extends an invitation to engage with the essence of cocoa and chocolate, enriching one's culinary repertoire with three distinctive recipes.

For the author, success isn't solely measured in the tangible outcomes of the dishes but also in the intangible moments of creativity, connection, and remembrance that these recipes evoke. This perspective makes the book a unique addition to the reader's kitchen journey.

For the home cook, the book serves as an inspiration to elevate home entertaining, offering a diverse palette ranging from interpreting timeless cocoa classics to embracing avant-garde creations. For professional chefs, it acts as a reference for innovative culinary expression, providing a springboard for experimentation, menu expansion, and the creation of unforgettable dining experiences that seamlessly blend tradition with contemporary flair.

The intentional formatting aligns with the author's vision, making each page a standalone recipe accessible to home cooks without formal training. Varying font sizes, kerning, and spacing are strategically employed to create a unique visual rhythm, enhancing the reader's experience. While acknowledging the potential for a future design masterpiece with an emphasis on photography and typography, the current irregular formatting serves as compressed notes and formulas, offering an unexpected and innovative approach to culinary guidance.

Note on Dark Chocolate:

When incorporating 'dark' chocolate into the following recipes, consider the following guidelines:

- 60-70% Dark Chocolate: This range provides a good balance of sweetness and chocolate intensity, suitable for recipes where the chocolate flavor should complement rather than dominate the dish.

- 70-75% Dark Chocolate: This range offers a more intense chocolate flavor with a slightly bitter undertone, ideal for recipes where a robust chocolate presence is desired, especially in savory applications.

- Above 75% Dark Chocolate: For those who appreciate a deep, intense chocolate flavor with minimal sweetness, a higher percentage is ideal. This works particularly well in rich, savory dishes.

The Savoury Chocolate Cookbook

Table of Contents

Dear Culinary Connoisseurs,

Embedded within the pages of this culinary compendium are approximately 140 recipes that redefine the art of gastronomy. Navigating between the realms of traditional and avant-garde savory chocolate creations, a selection of stand-out, inventive, deeply flavorful, and undeniably crowd-pleasing options invites you to embark on a culinary adventure like no other.

The expansive Mole Poblano, elevated to new heights with our Expanded Recipe, serves as a gateway to the rich history of Mexican cuisine. Alongside it, the Mole Verde with a Touch of Mexican Chocolate introduces the nuanced artistry of blending chocolate with vibrant green flavors.

Our exploration delves into the realm of chilis, offering creations like the Chipotle Chocolate Mole and the Spicy Dark Chocolate Turkey & Cactus Chili. In these dishes, the marriage of chocolate and spices creates symphonies for the taste buds. The complexities of Bourbon Molé Pulled Pork Tacos and Cognac, Dijon Mustard & Cocoa Braised Short Ribs beckon you to revel in the sublime marriage of spirits and cocoa.

Venturing into the world of pies, both savory and sweet, the Thai-inspired Peanut and Chocolate Zucchini Pie and the Chili Chocolate Beef Pie redefine the boundaries of traditional pastry with their inventive and crowd-pleasing allure.

Risottos become canvases for culinary innovation, featuring the Blue Cheese and Fig Chocolate Risotto and the Citrusy Chocolate Asparagus Risotto as testaments to the art of balancing sweet and savory notes.

The exploration extends to rubs and marinades with offerings like the Cherry Cocoa Rub and Mayan Cocoa-Rub, where chocolate transforms into an aromatic seasoning, enhancing every dish it graces.

In the realm of desserts, the Chocolate Tomato Jam Layer Cake, Bitter Chocolate No-Bake Cheesecake, and Chocolate Avocado Mousse with Sea Salt captivate the senses, showcasing the unforgettable symphony that the marriage of sweet and savory can create.

Our gastronomic odyssey concludes with a crescendo of flavor in Bourbon Molé Pulled Pork Tacos and Cognac, Dijon Mustard & Cocoa Braised Short Ribs. These dishes, born from the fusion of spirits, cocoa, and bold ingredients, represent the pinnacle of inventive, deeply flavorful, and crowd-pleasing culinary craftsmanship.

Within these pages, you'll encounter not just recipes but a culinary manifesto that celebrates the extraordinary, the inventive, and the timeless. As you embark on this sensory journey, may these dishes tantalize your taste buds, ignite your culinary passions, and leave an indelible mark on your gastronomic memory.

Savor the extraordinary!

The Savoury Chocolate Cookbook

The Recipes

Mole Poblano- Expanded Recipe

Mole Poblano, a distinguished masterpiece in Mexican culinary artistry, intricately weaves a rich tapestry of tradition and history deeply rooted in the cultural mosaic of Puebla. Legend has it that 17th-century nuns crafted the inaugural *Mole Poblano* to honor a visiting archbishop, skillfully blending indigenous, Spanish, and Afro-Mexican influences. This complex sauce, boasting over 30 ingredients, stands as a true embodiment of Mexico's diverse culinary heritage.

In *Mole Poblano*, a symphony of flavors unfolds as toasted chilies and aromatic spices harmonize with the bittersweet richness of chocolate. This transcendent sauce, initially born from humble beginnings, has evolved into a symbol of celebration, gracing festive occasions such as weddings and holidays. By embracing both ancestral roots and colonial legacies, *Mole Poblano* serves as a testament to the enduring fusion of cultures within Mexican gastronomy.

Ingredients

- 4 dried ancho chilies
- 3 dried mulato chilies
- 3 dried pasilla chilies
- 1/4 cup sesame seeds
- 1/4 cup almonds
- 1/4 cup pumpkin seeds
- 1/4 cup peanuts
- 1/4 cup hazelnuts
- 1/4 cup cashews
- 1/4 cup raisins
- 1/4 cup dried apricots
- 1/4 cup prunes
- 1/4 cup dried figs
- 1/4 cup dried cranberries
- 1/4 cup dried currants
- 4 cloves garlic
- 1 onion, chopped
- 1/4 cup sesame oil
- 1/4 cup corn oil
- 1/4 cup olive oil
- 4 stale corn tortillas
- 1/4 cup masa harina (corn flour)
- 2 stale slices of bread
- 2 tomatoes, roasted
- 2 tomatillos, roasted
- 1 plantain, ripe
- 1/4 cup dark chocolate, grated
- 1/4 cup Mexican chocolate, grated
- 1/4 cup sugar
- 1/4 cup piloncillo (Mexican brown sugar)
- 1/4 cup apple cider vinegar
- 1/4 cup orange juice
- 1/4 cup tequila
- 1/4 cup mezcal
- 1/4 cup chicken broth
- 1/4 cup turkey or vegetable broth
- 1/4 cup unsweetened cocoa powder
- 1/4 cup ground cinnamon
- 1/4 tsp ground cloves
- 1/4 tsp ground allspice
- 1/4 tsp ground coriander
- 1/4 tsp ground anise
- 1/4 tsp ground cardamom
- 1/4 tsp ground ginger
- 1/4 tsp dried thyme
- 1/4 tsp dried oregano

Mole Poblano- Expanded Recipe (continued)

The journey of this dish is characterized by its adaptability, seamlessly integrating into contemporary kitchens. *Mole Poblano* has evolved into a versatile addition, enhancing tacos, enchiladas, and even inspiring innovative fusion creations. The culinary legacy of Puebla, skillfully blending history and diverse influences, persists in the enduring popularity of *Mole Poblano*—a timeless reflection of cultural synthesis and an integral part of the vibrant tapestry of Mexican gastronomy.

In its evolution, *Mole Poblano* remains a living legacy, showcasing the adaptability and enduring appeal of traditional Mexican cuisine. Its nuanced flavors and intricate history provide a glimpse into the cultural richness of Puebla, making it a culinary treasure that continues to captivate palates and preserve the essence of Mexico's gastronomic heritage.

Instructions

1. Remove seeds and stems from dried chilies, then briefly toast them in a hot skillet. Soak in hot water until softened.

2. Toast sesame seeds, almonds, and raisins separately. Grind all toasted ingredients into a smooth paste.

3. In a large skillet, sauté chopped onions and garlic in a mixture of sesame, corn, and olive oil until softened.

4. Add all toasted nuts, seeds, and dried fruits to the onion and garlic mixture. Cook until lightly browned.

5. Incorporate torn tortillas and masa harina, cooking until they form a thick paste.

6. Blend roasted tomatoes, tomatillos, and ripe plantain. Add the puree to the skillet. Gradually introduce grated dark chocolate, Mexican chocolate, sugar, piloncillo, and all spices.

7. Pour in vinegar, orange juice, tequila, and mezcal. Stir in chicken and turkey (or vegetable) broth. Allow the mixture to simmer until it thickens.

8. Adjust the seasoning with salt and pepper. Adjust consistency with additional broth if needed.

9. Serve this opulent Mole Poblano over poultry, meats, or vegetables. This recipe makes 5-6 cups of Mole Poblano. It will keep 4-6 days in the refrigerator, tightly sealed.

Mole Poblano- Simplified Recipe

Crafting a simplified rendition of *Mole Poblano* offers a gateway to the rich tapestry of Mexican flavors without the intricacies. Streamlining the ingredients and cooking process beckons both novices and seasoned home cooks into a more accessible culinary journey, preserving the dish's authenticity. This simplified approach doesn't compromise on taste, ensuring a harmonious marriage of convenience and flavor in everyday cooking.

For those venturing into the complexities of the original recipe, this adaptation provides a practical entry point, embracing efficiency without sacrificing authenticity. To extend the lifespan of this culinary treasure, freezing portions in airtight containers ensures the enduring availability of authentic *Mole Poblano,* inviting enthusiasts to savor its flavors at their convenience.

Ingredients

- 4 dried ancho chilies
- 2 dried pasilla chilies
- 1/2 cup almonds
- 1/4 cup raisins
- 2 cloves garlic
- 1/4 tsp ground cinnamon
- 1/4 tsp ground cumin
- 1/4 tsp dried oregano
- 2 stale corn tortillas
- 2 oz Mexican chocolate
- 1/4 cup vegetable oil
- 1 onion, chopped
- 1 can (14 oz) diced tomatoes
- 4 cups chicken broth
- Salt to taste

Instructions

1. Remove seeds and stems from dried chilies, then toast them in a hot skillet for a minute. Soak in hot water until softened.

2. Toast almonds in the same skillet until golden. Set aside.

3. In a blender, combine soaked chilies, toasted almonds, raisins, garlic, cinnamon, cumin, oregano, torn tortillas, and chocolate. Blend into a smooth paste.

4. In a large pot, heat vegetable oil. Sauté chopped onion until translucent.

5. Pour the blended paste into the pot and cook for a few minutes, stirring continuously.

6. Add diced tomatoes and continue cooking until the mixture thickens.

7. Pour in chicken broth, bring to a simmer, and let it cook for 20-30 minutes until the flavors meld.

8. Add salt to taste. Serve the mole poblano over cooked chicken, turkey, or vegetables.

Mole Negro

Mole Negro, a sublime Oaxacan creation, unveils a history steeped in ancient culinary traditions. Rooted in pre-Hispanic Zapotec and Mixtec cultures, this complex sauce marries indigenous ingredients like chilies, chocolate, and indigenous herbs. Distinct from other moles, its depth arises from an array of dried chilies, including chilhuacle negro, giving it a dark, velvety hue. Mole Negro is traditionally associated with special occasions, weddings, and celebrations in Oaxaca, showcasing its elevated status in Mexican gastronomy.

Its bold, smoky flavor, derived from toasted chilies and intricate spice blends, sets it apart. Commonly served over poultry, Mole Negro's rich, nuanced taste reflects the diverse culinary heritage of Oaxaca, an ancient tribute to the symphony of flavors ingrained in Mexico's cultural tapestry.

Ingredients

- 4 dried chilhuacle negro chilies
- 4 dried mulato chilies
- 3 dried pasilla chilies
- 1/4 cup almonds
- 1/4 cup peanuts
- 1/4 cup sesame seeds
- 3 cloves garlic
- 1/2 cup raisins
- 1/4 cup masa harina (corn flour)
- 1/4 cup vegetable oil
- 2 stale corn tortillas
- 1/4 cup Mexican chocolate, grated
- 1/4 cup Oaxacan chocolate, grated
- 1 ripe plantain
- 1/4 cup lard
- 1 onion, chopped
- 3 tomatoes, roasted
- 2 tomatillos, roasted
- 2 cinnamon sticks
- 2 cloves
- 1/4 tsp ground black pepper
- 1/4 tsp ground cumin
- 1/4 tsp dried thyme
- Salt to taste
- 4 cups chicken broth

Instructions

1. Soak dried chilies until soft. Toast almonds, peanuts, and sesame seeds until golden. Blend soaked chilies, nuts, seeds, garlic, raisins, masa harina, and water into a smooth paste.

2. Heat oil, add paste, and cook until thick. Stir in grated Mexican and Oaxacan chocolate, and the ripe plantain until melted.

3. In a separate pan, sauté chopped onion in lard, add roasted tomatoes, tomatillos, spices, and herbs. Blend until smooth.

4. Add aromatic blend to the pot with the chili-chocolate mixture. Pour in chicken broth, simmer for 30-40 minutes until thick.

5. This recipe produces approximately 4 to 5 cups of Mole Negro

Mole Coloradito

Mole Coloradito, a jewel of Oaxacan cuisine, draws from the region's ancient culinary tapestry. Its reddish-brown brilliance mirrors the fertile Oaxacan soil, celebrating a rich blend of earthy chilies, tomatoes, and spices. Distinct from other moles, *Coloradito* presents a milder yet intricately balanced flavor profile. Rooted in Zapotec and Mixtec traditions, each ingredient is chosen for its historical significance, weaving a narrative of cultural heritage.

This versatile mole, often paired with poultry, transcends the ordinary, gracing both festive occasions and everyday meals with its profound richness. *Mole Coloradito* encapsulates the artistry of Oaxacan gastronomy, a living testament to the enduring traditions and flavors that captivate palates across generations, offering a delectable journey into the heart of Oaxacan culinary excellence.

Ingredients

- 4 guajillo chilies
- 3 ancho chilies
- 2 cloves garlic
- 1/2 onion, chopped
- 1/2 tsp cumin seeds
- 1/2 tsp black peppercorns
- 1/2 tsp coriander seeds
- 1/2 tsp dried thyme
- 1/2 tsp dried oregano
- 1/4 cup almonds
- 1/4 cup peanuts
- 1/4 cup sesame seeds
- 2 stale corn tortillas
- 2 tomatoes, roasted
- 1 tomatillo, roasted
- 1/2 ripe plantain
- 1/4 cup lard or vegetable oil
- 4 cups chicken broth
- 1/4 cup Mexican chocolate, grated
- Salt to taste

Instructions

1. Soak guajillo and ancho chilies until soft.

2. Toast almonds, peanuts, and sesame seeds until golden.

3. Blend soaked chilies, nuts, seeds, garlic, onion, cumin, peppercorns, coriander, thyme, oregano, torn tortillas, roasted tomatoes, tomatillo, ripe plantain, and grated Mexican chocolate into a smooth paste.

4. Sauté the paste in lard or vegetable oil until thickened.

5. Pour in chicken broth and simmer for 20-30 minutes.

6. Season with salt to taste. This recipe is designed to make approximately 4-5 cups of mole sauce.

Mole Amarillo

Mole Amarillo, a radiant tribute to Oaxacan gastronomy, embodies the vivid flavors of the region. Its golden hue, reminiscent of the sun-drenched landscapes, stems from a blend of guajillo and costeño chilies, complemented by aromatic spices. Unlike its darker counterparts, Amarillo features a lighter, zestier profile, showcasing the vibrancy of Oaxacan ingredients. Traditionally paired with poultry, this mole offers a tantalizing harmony of heat and citrusy brightness. Rooted in ancient culinary traditions, *Mole Amarillo* reflects the cultural diversity of Oaxaca, a testament to the region's ability to weave history into contemporary dining experiences. Whether gracing festive celebrations or everyday meals, *Mole Amarillo* stands as a testament to the dynamic and flavorful essence of Oaxacan cuisine. Our variation adds an extra layer of richness with 1/8th cup of grated Mexican chocolate..

Ingredients

- 4 guajillo chilies
- 4 costeño chilies
- 2 cloves garlic
- 1/2 onion, chopped
- 1/2 tsp cumin seeds
- 1/2 tsp black peppercorns
- 1/2 tsp coriander seeds
- 1/2 tsp dried thyme
- 1/2 tsp dried oregano
- 1/4 cup almonds
- 1/4 cup pumpkin seeds
- 1/4 cup sesame seeds
- 2 stale corn tortillas
- 2 tomatoes, roasted
- 1 tomatillo, roasted
- 1/2 ripe plantain
- 1/4 cup lard or vegetable oil
- 4 cups chicken broth
- 1/8 cup Mexican chocolate, grated
- Salt to taste

Instructions

1. Remove seeds and stems from guajillo and costeño chilies. Toast until fragrant, then soak in hot water until soft.

2. Toast almonds, pumpkin seeds, and sesame seeds until golden.

3. Blend soaked chilies, toasted nuts and seeds, garlic, onion, cumin seeds, black peppercorns, coriander seeds, thyme, oregano, torn tortillas, roasted tomatoes, roasted tomatillo, ripe plantain, and grated Mexican chocolate into a smooth paste.

4. Heat lard or vegetable oil in a pot. Add the paste and cook until thickened.

6. Pour in chicken broth and simmer for 20-30 minutes. Add salt to taste. This recipe is designed to make approximately 4-5 cups of mole sauce.

Mole Verde with a Touch of Mexican Chocolate

Mole Verde, a cherished component of Mexican cuisine, originates from Oaxaca, celebrating the region's bounty of fresh green ingredients. This verdant mole stands out for its vibrant flavors derived from tomatillos, green chilies, herbs, and seeds. Unlike its richer, darker counterparts, Mole Verde boasts a lighter, herbaceous profile, traditionally paired with poultry or pork. As culinary traditions evolve, we explore a contemporary twist with a new *Mole Verde* variation featuring a touch of Mexican chocolate. This addition introduces a subtle richness and depth, elevating the mole's complexity while preserving its bright, herbal essence. The marriage of traditional and innovative elements in this Mole Verde variation captures the dynamic spirit of Mexican gastronomy, offering a delightful fusion of classic flavors with a modern touch.

Ingredients

- 8 tomatillos, husked and washed
- 3 poblano chilies
- 2 jalapeño chilies
- 2 cloves garlic
- 1/2 onion, chopped
- 1/2 cup fresh cilantro, chopped
- 1/4 cup fresh parsley, chopped
- 1/4 cup fresh epazote leaves (optional)
- 1/4 cup pumpkin seeds
- 1/4 cup sesame seeds
- 1/4 cup almonds
- 2 tbsp Mexican chocolate, grated
- 2 tbsp lard or vegetable oil
- 4 cups chicken or vegetable broth
- Salt to taste

Instructions

1. Roast poblano and jalapeño chilies until charred. Peel, remove seeds, and chop.

2. Blend tomatillos, roasted chilies, garlic, onion, cilantro, parsley, epazote (if using), pumpkin seeds, sesame seeds, almonds, and grated Mexican chocolate into a smooth paste.

3. Sauté paste in lard or vegetable oil until thickened.

4. Pour in chicken or vegetable broth and simmer for 15-20 minutes.

5. Add salt to taste.

6. Serve or save. This recipe is designed to make approximately 4 cups of mole sauce.

Mole Almendrado with Mexican Cocoa

Mole Almendrado, a revered creation in Mexican culinary heritage, boasts a rich history originating in Oaxaca, blending indigenous ingredients with Spanish influence. Celebrated for its velvety texture and nutty undertones, *Mole Almendrado* is a staple in festive occasions. Distinct from other moles, it stands out for its emphasis on almonds, incorporating their creamy essence. Traditionally paired with poultry, its versatility also graces pork or beef dishes. As we innovate, we introduce a novel Mexican cocoa variation to *Mole Almendrado*. This addition, echoing ancient Mesoamerican traditions, infuses a nuanced chocolatey depth. Balancing the richness of almonds with the subtle bitterness of Mexican cocoa, this variation enhances the mole's complexity, offering a delightful fusion of traditional flavors with a contemporary twist, making it a tantalizing addition to diverse culinary experiences.

Ingredients

- 4 dried ancho chilies
- 1 cup almonds
- 2 cloves garlic
- 1/2 onion, chopped
- 1/2 cup sesame seeds
- 1/4 cup raisins
- 1/4 cup Mexican cocoa powder
- 2 tbsp lard or vegetable oil
- 4 cups chicken or vegetable broth
- Salt to taste

Instructions

1. Soak ancho chilies until soft. Blend soaked chilies, almonds, garlic, onion, sesame seeds, raisins, and Mexican cocoa powder into a smooth paste.

2. Heat lard or vegetable oil in a pot. Sauté the paste until it thickens.

3. Pour in chicken or vegetable broth and simmer for 15-20 minutes.

4. Add salt to taste.

5. Serve the Mole Almendrado with a touch of Mexican cocoa over cooked poultry, pork, or your preferred protein. This recipe is designed to make approximately 4 cups of mole sauce.

Mole Chichilo with Mexican Cocoa

Mole Chichilo, originating in Oaxaca, is a revered member of Mexico's rich mole tradition. Distinguished by its unique blend of guajillo and pasilla chilies, thyme, oregano, and the intriguing addition of ripe plantains, it showcases Oaxacan ingenuity. Known for its intense and aromatic flavors, it traditionally accompanies meats like beef or lamb. Unlike its counterparts, *Mole Chichilo* boasts a darker, smokier profile.

In our exploration, we introduce a novel Mexican cocoa variation, infusing the mole with a deep and bold chocolate essence. The cocoa's bitter notes harmonize with the earthy spices, creating a symphony of flavors that adds a contemporary twist to this traditional dish. This innovative approach pays homage to the dynamic nature of Mexican gastronomy, inviting culinary enthusiasts to savor the intricate balance of tradition and experimentation in every savory bite.

Ingredients

- 5 dried guajillo chilies
- 3 dried pasilla chilies
- 3 cloves garlic
- 1/2 onion, chopped
- 1/2 tsp cumin seeds
- 1/2 tsp black peppercorns
- 1/2 tsp coriander seeds
- 1/2 tsp dried thyme
- 1/2 tsp dried oregano
- 1/4 cup almonds
- 1/4 cup peanuts
- 1/4 cup sesame seeds
- 2 ripe plantains
- 1/4 cup lard or vegetable oil
- 4 cups beef or vegetable broth
- 2 tbsp cocoa powder
- Salt to taste

Instructions

1. Soak guajillo and pasilla chilies until soft.

2. Toast almonds, peanuts, and sesame seeds until golden. Blend soaked chilies, toasted nuts and seeds, garlic, onion, cumin seeds, black peppercorns, coriander seeds, thyme, oregano, and ripe plantains with cocoa powder into a smooth paste.

3. Sauté paste in lard or vegetable oil until thickened.

4. Pour in beef or vegetable broth and simmer for 20-30 minutes.

5. Add salt to taste. Serve or save. This recipe is designed to make approximately 4 cups of mole sauce.

Mole de Xico

Mole de Xico, originating from the culinary gem of *Xico,* unfolds a tale of Mexico's diverse gastronomic heritage. Infused with the essence of toasted nuts, chilies, and aromatic spices, this mole transcends tradition. Our rendition, a contemporary twist, introduces a subtle hint of cocoa, a nuanced celebration of culinary evolution.

Historically enjoyed during festivities, *Mole de Xico* offers a rich complement to poultry or meats. This modern interpretation pays homage to the region's profound culinary legacy, seamlessly intertwining ancient practices with a touch of cocoa sophistication. Embark on a savory journey, savoring the harmonious fusion of tradition and innovation in every delightful bite.

Ingredients

- 4 dried ancho chilies
- 3 dried pasilla chilies
- 1/2 cup almonds
- 1/4 cup peanuts
- 1/4 cup raisins
- 2 cloves garlic
- 1/2 onion, chopped
- 1/4 cup sesame seeds
- 1/4 cup pumpkin seeds
- 1/2 tsp black pepper
- 1/2 tsp cumin seeds
- 1/2 tsp coriander seeds
- 1/4 tsp cloves
- 1/4 tsp cinnamon
- 1/4 tsp dried thyme
- 1/4 tsp dried oregano
- 2 tbsp unsweetened cocoa powder
- 4 cups chicken or vegetable broth
- 2 tbsp lard or vegetable oil
- Salt to taste

Instructions

1. Remove seeds and stems from ancho and pasilla chilies. Toast, then soak in hot water until soft.

2. Toast almonds, peanuts, sesame seeds, and pumpkin seeds until golden.

3. Blend soaked chilies, toasted nuts and seeds, raisins, garlic, onion, black pepper, cumin seeds, coriander seeds, cloves, cinnamon, thyme, oregano, and cocoa powder into a smooth paste.

4. Heat lard or vegetable oil in a pot. Add the paste and cook over medium heat until thickened.

5. Pour in chicken or vegetable broth. Simmer for 20-30 minutes, allowing flavors to meld. Add salt to taste.

6. Serve, refrigerate or freeze.

Mole Manchamantel- Expanded Recipe

Mole Manchamantel, a jewel in the culinary crown of Mexico, unfolds a captivating narrative of evolution and innovation. Its origins rooted in Oaxaca, this exquisite mole tells the tale of indigenous brilliance, weaving together a symphony of dried chilies, nuts, seeds, and aromatic spices that resonate with the rich history of Mexican cuisine.

Renowned for its distinct sweet and savory profile, *Mole Manchamantel* becomes a harmonious dance partner for various proteins, especially the slow-cooked splendor of pork. Our contemporary twist introduces an enchanting element – the infusion of bittersweet or Mexican chocolate. This addition pays homage to the historical significance of chocolate in Mexican culinary traditions, adding a layer of velvety richness and profound cocoa undertones to the mole.

Ingredients

Chili Paste:
- 4 dried ancho chilies
- 3 dried guajillo chilies
- 2 dried chipotle chilies
- 3 cloves garlic
- 1/2 onion, chopped

Nuts and Seeds:
- 1/4 cup almonds
- 1/4 cup peanuts
- 1/4 cup sesame seeds

Fruits and Sweet Elements:
- 1/4 cup raisins
- 1/4 cup dried apricots
- 1/4 cup tomatoes, diced
- 1/4 cup pineapple, diced
- 1/4 cup plantain, ripe and diced

Aromatics and Spices:
- 1 cinnamon stick
- 2 cloves
- 1/2 tsp cumin seeds
- 1/2 tsp coriander seeds
- 1/2 tsp dried thyme
- 1/2 tsp dried oregano

Additional Ingredients:
- 1/4 cup lard
- 4 cups chicken or vegetable broth
- 2 tbsp chocolate, grated
(bittersweet or Mexican chocolate)
- 1/4 cup red wine vinegar
- 2 tbsp sugar (adjust to taste)
- Salt to taste
- Freshly ground black pepper to taste

Mole Manchamantel - Expanded Recipe (continued)

In embracing this unique variation, we honor the enduring spirit of Mexican gastronomy, seamlessly blending centuries-old traditions with a dash of modern ingenuity. *Mole Manchamantel* transforms into a canvas where flavors from bygone eras seamlessly converge with the present, inviting culinary enthusiasts on a sensory journey that exalts the vibrant and ever-evolving essence of Mexican culinary heritage.

As the flavors intermingle in each tantalizing bite, the dish transcends its role as a mere symbol of tradition. Instead, *Mole Manchamantel* stands tall as a living testament to the dynamic creativity pulsating through the heart of Mexican gastronomy, beckoning enthusiasts to savor a dish that encapsulates the captivating narrative etched in every spoonful.

Instructions

1. Remove seeds and stems from ancho, guajillo, and chipotle chilies. Toast until fragrant, then soak in hot water until soft.

2. Toast almonds, peanuts, and sesame seeds until golden.

3. In a blender, combine soaked chilies, garlic, onion, toasted nuts and seeds, cinnamon stick, cloves, cumin seeds, coriander seeds, thyme, and oregano. Blend into a smooth paste.

4. Heat lard in a pot. Add the chili paste and cook over medium heat until it thickens.

5. Incorporate raisins, dried apricots, tomatoes, pineapple, plantain, and the aromatic spices (cinnamon, cloves, cumin, coriander, thyme, oregano). Stir to meld the flavors.

6. Pour in chicken or vegetable broth, red wine vinegar, and sugar. Simmer for 30-40 minutes, allowing the flavors to develop.

7. Add grated chocolate to the mole, stirring until fully melted and integrated.

8. Salt and freshly ground black pepper to taste. Adjust sugar if needed for a balanced flavor.

9. This recipe yields approximately 4 to 6 cups of Mole Manchamantel sauce.Serve or freeze according to use and/or instructions.

Mole de Cacahuate

Mole de Cacahuate, a cherished Mexican culinary creation, represents a fascinating evolution of traditional moles. Rooted in the rich culinary tapestry of Mexico, this mole showcases an ingenious blend of roasted peanuts, chocolate, and aromatic spices.

Unlike its counterparts, the star of *Mole de Cacahuate* is the humble peanut, imparting a distinct nutty flavor and creamy texture. This variation pays homage to the diverse culinary landscape of Mexico by incorporating elements of ancient and modern flavor profiles. Our unique twist introduces the richness of dark chocolate, elevating the mole's complexity and creating a harmonious marriage of nutty, chocolatey, and savory notes. *Mole de Cacahuate* stands as a testament to the ongoing innovation within Mexican gastronomy, offering a delightful departure from the traditional mole experience.

Ingredients

- 4 dried ancho chilies
- 3 dried guajillo chilies
- 1 cup roasted peanuts
- 1/4 cup sesame seeds
- 3 cloves garlic
- 1/2 onion, chopped
- 1/2 cup raisins
- 1/4 cup masa harina (corn flour)
- 1/4 cup smooth peanut butter
- 1/4 cup dark chocolate, grated
- 1 cinnamon stick
- 3 cloves
- 1/2 tsp cumin seeds
- 1/2 tsp coriander seeds
- 1/2 tsp dried thyme
- 1/2 tsp dried oregano
- 4 cups chicken or vegetable broth
- 1/4 cup vegetable oil
- Salt and pepper to taste

Instructions

1. Remove seeds and stems from ancho and guajillo chilies. Toast, then soak in hot water until soft.

2. Toast peanuts and sesame seeds until golden.

3. Blend soaked chilies, peanuts, sesame seeds, garlic, onion, raisins, masa harina, peanut butter, grated chocolate, spices, and herbs into a smooth paste.

4. Heat vegetable oil in a pot. Add the chili paste and cook until thickened.

5. Pour in chicken or vegetable broth. Simmer for 20-30 minutes. And, season with salt and pepper.

6. Ladle Mole de Cacahuate over cooked protein.

Chipotle Chocolate Mole

Hailing from the rich tapestry of Mexican cuisine, our Chipotle Chocolate Mole is a contemporary twist on traditional moles, boasting a unique fusion of smoky chipotle, rich dark chocolate, and an array of aromatic spices. Rooted in the profound culinary history of mole, this recipe pays homage to the indigenous flavors of chipotle peppers and the ancient use of chocolate in Mexican gastronomy.

Distinguished by its versatility, this mole transcends traditional boundaries, elevating dishes beyond the customary seafood pairing. Its bold and smoky profile harmonizes flawlessly with chicken, pork, and even vegetarian options, offering a tantalizing experience with every bite. This modern mole variation stands as a testament to the dynamic evolution of Mexican culinary heritage, inviting enthusiasts to savor a contemporary twist on a classic masterpiece.

Ingredients

- 4 dried chipotle chilies
- 3 dried ancho chilies
- 1/2 cup almonds
- 1/4 cup sesame seeds
- 3 cloves garlic
- 1/2 onion, chopped
- 1/4 cup raisins
- 1/4 cup dark chocolate, grated
- 1 tsp cumin seeds
- 1 tsp coriander seeds
- 1/2 tsp cinnamon
- 1/2 tsp dried thyme
- 1/2 tsp dried oregano
- 4 cups fish or vegetable broth
- 2 tbsp olive oil
- Salt to taste

Instructions

1. Soak and blend chipotle and ancho chilies with almonds, sesame seeds, garlic, onion, raisins, dark chocolate, cumin seeds, coriander seeds, cinnamon, thyme, and oregano.

2. Toast almonds and sesame seeds until golden.

3. Heat olive oil in a pot and cook the paste until thickened.

4. Pour in fish or vegetable broth and simmer for 20-30 minutes.

5. Season with salt.

Espresso-Infused Almond Mole

Steeped in the rich tapestry of Mexican culinary heritage, the Espresso-Infused Almond Mole is a contemporary marvel, embodying the fusion of traditional ingredients with a modern twist. Rooted in the historic reverence for mole, this unique variation takes inspiration from the bold flavors of espresso and the nutty essence of almonds. The marriage of dark chocolate, ancho chilies, and the aromatic spices with a shot of freshly brewed espresso creates a symphony of flavors that elevates the mole experience.

Distinguishing itself from its counterparts, this mole presents a robust and nutty profile, making it an ideal companion for grilled meats like pork or duck. The Espresso-Infused Almond Mole stands as a testament to the ever-evolving nature of Mexican cuisine, where tradition and innovation converge to create culinary masterpieces.

Ingredients

- 4 dried ancho chilies
- 1/2 cup almonds
- 1/4 cup sesame seeds
- 3 cloves garlic
- 1/2 onion, chopped
- 1/4 cup raisins
- 1/4 cup dark chocolate, grated
- 1 shot of freshly brewed espresso
- 1 tsp cumin seeds
- 1 tsp coriander seeds
- 1/2 tsp cinnamon
- 1/2 tsp dried thyme
- 1/2 tsp dried oregano
- 4 cups chicken or vegetable broth
- 2 tbsp olive oil
- Salt to taste

Instructions

1. Soak ancho chilies and blend with almonds, sesame seeds, garlic, onion, raisins, dark chocolate, espresso, cumin seeds, coriander seeds, cinnamon, thyme, and oregano.

2. Toast almonds and sesame seeds until golden.

3. Cook paste in olive oil until thickened.

4. Pour in broth, simmer for 20-30 minutes.

5. Season with salt.

6. Pairs wonderfully with pork tamales and duck tacos. Serve, freeze or refrigerate for 4-5 days in airtight container.

Sour Cherry Chocolate Mole

Rooted in the traditional complexities of Mexican mole, the Sour Cherry Chocolate Mole seamlessly integrates the tangy allure of sour cherries with the rich, bittersweet notes of dark chocolate. This unique mole is a contemporary celebration of contrasts, bringing together sweet, sour, and savory in a harmonious dance of flavors. Diverging from traditional moles, its vibrant profile offers versatility, enhancing both savory and sweet dishes. The sour cherry infusion creates a tantalizing twist that pairs exceptionally well with grilled meats, roasted vegetables, and even dessert nachos. Embracing experimentation within the mole tradition, the term 'mole' transcends a specific recipe, evolving into a classification that accommodates innovative fusions. This culinary exploration showcases the adaptability of mole, inviting enthusiasts to experience the dynamic evolution of a beloved Mexican culinary heritage.

Ingredients

- 4 dried ancho chilies
- 1 cup sour cherry preserves
- 1/2 cup dark chocolate, grated
- 3 cloves garlic
- 1/2 onion, chopped
- 1/4 cup almonds
- 1/4 cup sesame seeds
- 1 tsp cumin seeds
- 1 tsp coriander seeds
- 1/2 tsp cinnamon
- 1/2 tsp dried thyme
- 1/2 tsp dried oregano
- 4 cups chicken or vegetable broth
- 2 tbsp olive oil
- Salt to taste

Instructions

1. Remove seeds and stems from ancho chilies. Toast until fragrant, then soak in hot water until soft.

2. In a dry pan, toast almonds and sesame seeds until golden.

3. In a blender, combine soaked chilies, sour cherry preserves, grated dark chocolate, garlic, onion, almonds, sesame seeds, cumin seeds, coriander seeds, cinnamon, thyme, and oregano. Blend into a smooth paste.

4. Heat olive oil in a pot. Add the paste and cook over medium heat until it thickens.

5. Pour in chicken or vegetable broth. Simmer for 20-30 minutes, allowing the flavors to meld.

6. Season with salt to taste.

Smoky Chocolate Mole

The Smoky Chocolate Mole is a contemporary invention, marrying tradition and innovation. Emerging from the ancestral kitchens, it features ancho and chipotle chilies, elevated by a symphony of luxurious elements. The blend of cocoa, dark chocolate, almonds, and sesame seeds results in a velvety richness, while raisins and mezcal add complexity. This recipe is an homage to the culinary tapestry of Mexico, celebrating the evolution of mole.

Upon tasting, anticipate a dance of smoky, spicy, and bittersweet flavors, harmonized by the depth of dried thyme. This unique mole transforms into a lavish sauce for grilled meats, a decadent dip for churros, or a gourmet addition to traditional dishes. A culinary masterpiece, the Smoky Chocolate Mole mirrors the evolution of Mexican cuisine, offering an indulgent journey through time and flavor.

Ingredients

- 2 tbsp high-quality cocoa powder
3 oz high-% dark chocolate (70% cocoa or higher), finely chopped
- 3 dried ancho chilies, deseeded and rehydrated
- 2 dried chipotle chilies, deseeded and rehydrated
1/4 cup almonds, toasted and finely ground
- 1/4 cup sesame seeds, toasted
- 1/4 cup premium EVOO
- 1 large onion, finely chopped
- 4 cloves garlic, minced
- 1 tsp smoked paprika
- 1 tsp ground cumin
- 1 tsp ground cinnamon
- 1 tsp dried thyme
- 1/4 cup raisins
- 1/4 cup premium mezcal
- 3 cups rich chicken or veg broth
- 1 cup strong brewed coffee
- Salt and freshly ground black pepper to taste

Instructions

1. Blend cocoa powder, dark chocolate, re-hydrated ancho chilies, chipotle chilies, ground almonds, and toasted sesame seeds until smooth.

2. In a saucepan, sauté chopped onion in EVOO until translucent. Add minced garlic and sauté for 1 more minute.

3. Stir in the chocolate-chili paste, cooking for 2-3 minutes.

4. Add smoked paprika, cumin, cinnamon, dried thyme, and raisins.

4. Pour in mezcal, chicken or veg broth, and strong coffee. Simmer for 25-30 minutes until the sauce thickens.

5. Season with salt and freshly ground black pepper to taste.

Fig and Chocolate Mole

Crafting this Fig and Chocolate Mole was a deliberate fusion of respect for the rich traditions of Mexican mole and a desire for contemporary innovation. We meticulously balanced the earthy heat of rehydrated ancho and chipotle chilies with the nutty creaminess of ground almonds and toasted sesame seeds, forming a base that pays homage to classic mole complexity. Introducing figs and dark chocolate elevated the profile, infusing a luxurious sweetness that complements the deep flavors. The addition of premium tequila and dark beer brought a nuanced richness, expanding the culinary narrative.

This mole resonates with the essence of Mexican mole, celebrating its intricate tapestry while embracing new dimensions. It pairs seamlessly with grilled meats, enchiladas, or roasted vegetables, offering a versatile canvas for culinary exploration. In its harmonious blend of tradition and innovation, this Fig and Chocolate Mole invites a cross-cultural celebration at the dining table.

Ingredients

- 2 tablespoons vegetable oil
- 1 medium onion, finely chopped
- 4 cloves garlic, minced
- 3 dried ancho chilies, deseeded and rehydrated
- 2 dried chipotle chilies, deseeded and rehydrated
- 1/4 cup almonds, toasted and finely ground
- 1/4 cup sesame seeds, toasted
- 1/4 cup premium extra virgin olive oil
- 1 teaspoon ground cumin
- 1 teaspoon ground coriander
- 1 teaspoon smoked paprika
- 1 teaspoon dried oregano
- 1/4 cup raisins
- 1/4 cup premium tequila
- 3 cups dark beer (stout or porter)
- 1 cup rich chicken or vegetable broth
- 3 ounces high-quality dark chocolate (70% cocoa or higher), finely chopped
- 1/2 cup dried figs, chopped
- Salt and pepper to taste

Instructions

1. Blend rehydrated ancho chilies, chipotle chilies, ground almonds, and toasted sesame seeds with enough water until smooth.

2. In a saucepan, heat olive oil over medium heat. Sauté chopped onion until translucent, add minced garlic, and sauté for 1 minute.

3. Add the chili-nut paste to the saucepan, stir for 2-3 minutes. Incorporate ground cumin, coriander, smoked paprika, and dried oregano. Add raisins and tequila, simmer for 2 minutes, then pour in dark beer and broth. Simmer for 20 minutes.

4. Introduce chopped figs and dark chocolate. Stir until chocolate is melted, letting figs infuse sweetness. Season with salt and freshly ground black pepper to taste.

Tequila Sunset Mole, or
Blood Orange, Tequila and Chocolate Mole

The Tequila Sunset Mole pays homage to Mexican culinary heritage with a contemporary twist. Originating from ancestral flavors, it artfully marries ancho chilies, epazote, and blood oranges, reflecting a rich historical background. Crafted for modern tastes, this unique mole introduces tequila, dark chocolate, and a blend of dried fruits, elevating the traditional recipe.

On the palate, experience the luxurious interplay of premium tequila, the subtle heat of ancho chilies, and the bittersweet depth of dark chocolate. The dried fruits add a chewy texture, enhancing the symphony of flavors. Versatile and innovative, this mole transforms into a celestial drizzle for fruits, a lavish sauce for proteins, or a decadent topping for desserts, showcasing the evolution of timeless Mexican cuisine.

Ingredients

- 2 tablespoons lard
- 1 medium red onion, finely chopped
- 4 cloves garlic, minced
- 3 dried ancho chilies, de-seeded and re-hydrated
- 2 teaspoons dried epazote
- 1/4 cup high-quality dark chocolate (70% cocoa or higher), finely chopped
- 1/4 cup mixed dried fruits (apricots, golden raisins, prunes), finely chopped
- 1/4 cup premium tequila
- 3 cups rich chicken or vegetable broth
- 1 cup fresh blood orange juice
- 1 teaspoon ground cinnamon
- 1 teaspoon ground cumin
- 1 teaspoon smoked paprika
- 1/4 cup toasted sesame seeds
- Salt and freshly ground black pepper to taste

Instructions

1. Heat vegetable oil in a saucepan over medium heat. Sauté chopped red onion until translucent, then add minced garlic and sauté for 1 more minute.

2. In a blender, combine re-hydrated ancho chilies, dried epazote, dark chocolate, mixed dried fruits, and tequila. Blend into a smooth paste.

3. Add the paste to the saucepan, stir for 2-3 minutes.

4. Pour in broth and blood orange juice. Stir in ground cinnamon, cumin, smoked paprika, and toasted sesame seeds.

5. Simmer for 25-30 minutes until the sauce thickens.

6. Season with salt and freshly ground black pepper to taste.

Cerveza Obscura Cocoa Mole

This recipe ingeniously leverages the rich tradition of Mexican mole, skillfully weaving a cross-cultural contemporary fusion. By combining traditional elements with modern twists, it transforms into a tantalizing sauce that transcends culinary boundaries. The base, featuring rehydrated ancho and chipotle chilies, toasted almonds, and sesame seeds, mirrors the essence of authentic mole. Elevating the experience, premium tequila and dark beer infuse complexity, while the addition of high-quality dark chocolate enhances depth.

The marriage of cumin, coriander, smoked paprika, and dried oregano adds layers of flavor, harmonizing with the sweet notes of raisins. This bold concoction, simmered to perfection, finds balance in the interplay of textures and tastes. Pairing exquisitely with various dishes, it invites experimentation—be it drizzled over grilled meats, nestled alongside roasted vegetables, or accompanying hearty grains. A testament to culinary innovation, this cross-cultural masterpiece embarks on a journey, blending tradition with the avant-garde in every savory drop.

Ingredients

- 2 tablespoons vegetable oil
- 1 medium onion, finely chopped
- 4 cloves garlic, minced
- 3 dried ancho chilies, deseeded and rehydrated
- 2 dried chipotle chilies, deseeded and rehydrated
- 1/4 cup almonds, toasted and finely ground
- 1/4 cup sesame seeds, toasted
- 1/4 cup premium extra virgin olive oil
- 1 teaspoon ground cumin
- 1 teaspoon ground coriander
- 1 teaspoon smoked paprika
- 1 teaspoon dried oregano
- 1/4 cup raisins
- 1/4 cup premium tequila
- 3 cups dark beer (stout or porter)
- 1 cup rich chicken or vegetable broth
- 3 ounces high-quality dark chocolate (70% cocoa or higher), finely chopped
--Salt and pepper to taste

Instructions

1. Blend rehydrated ancho chilies, chipotle chilies, ground almonds, toasted sesame seeds, and enough water until smooth.

2. In a saucepan, heat olive oil over medium heat. Sauté chopped onion until translucent, add minced garlic, and sauté for 1 minute.

3. Add the chili-nut paste to the saucepan, stir for 2-3 minutes. Stir in ground cumin, coriander, smoked paprika, and dried oregano. Add raisins and tequila, let it simmer for 2 minutes, then pour in dark beer and broth. Simmer for 20 minutes.

Stir in chopped dark chocolate until melted, and add salt and freshly ground black pepper to taste.

Pistachio Chocolate Mole

Crafting this Pistachio Chocolate Mole was a whimsical exploration, respecting the core concept of Mexican mole while injecting a playful spirit. By blending rehydrated ancho and chipotle chilies with toasted pistachios and sesame seeds, we curated a unique harmony of flavors that adds a cheerful twist to tradition. This innovative mole pays homage to Mexican culinary heritage while embracing modern creativity. The incorporation of raisins, tequila, and dark chocolate elevates the complexity, presenting a symphony of sweet, smoky, and nutty notes.

This mole resonates with the soul of Mexican cuisine, expanding its horizons with a joyful palette. Pair it liberally: drizzle over grilled meats, spoon onto enchiladas, or let it accompany roasted vegetables for a lively burst of flavors. In each bite, savor the fusion of respect for tradition and the excitement of our shared playground of culinary innovation.

Ingredients

- 2 tablespoons vegetable oil
- 1 medium onion, finely chopped
- 4 cloves garlic, minced
- 3 dried ancho chilies, deseeded and rehydrated
- 2 dried chipotle chilies, deseeded and rehydrated
- 1/2 cup shelled pistachios, toasted and finely ground
- 1/4 cup sesame seeds, toasted
- 1/4 cup premium extra virgin olive oil
- 1 teaspoon ground cumin
- 1 teaspoon ground coriander
- 1 teaspoon smoked paprika
- 1 teaspoon dried oregano
- 1/4 cup raisins
- 1/4 cup premium tequila
- 3 cups vegetable broth
- 3 ounces high-quality dark chocolate (70% cocoa or higher), finely chopped
- Salt and pepper to taste

Instructions

1. Blend soaked ancho chilies, chipotle chilies, toasted pistachios, and sesame seeds with water until smooth.

2. In a pan, heat olive oil. Cook onions until clear, add garlic, cook 1 minute.

3. Add the blended mix, stir 2-3 minutes. Add cumin, coriander, paprika, and oregano. Include raisins and tequila, simmer 2 minutes.

4. Pour in vegetable broth, simmer for 20 minutes.

5. Stir in chopped dark chocolate until melted. Season with salt and pepper to taste.

Maple Chocolate Mole

Rooted in the rich tradition of Mexican mole, the Maple Chocolate Mole introduces a semi-sweet complexity, fusing the robust flavors of dark chocolate with the nuanced sweetness of maple. This distinctive mole embodies a symphony of ingredients, featuring ancho and pasilla chilies for a smoky warmth. Ground cinnamon and cloves provide depth, while almonds contribute a nutty richness. The addition of pure maple syrup elevates the sweetness, balancing the bitter notes of chocolate.

This semi-sweet mole creates a luscious, velvety sauce that pairs exquisitely with slow-cooked meats such as braised pork or grilled chicken. As the maple undertones dance with the bittersweet chocolate, each bite unfolds a harmonious blend of flavors, inviting you to savor the intricate beauty of this contemporary twist on a classic culinary masterpiece.

Ingredients

- 4 dried ancho chilies
- 2 dried pasilla chilies
- 1 cup pure maple syrup
- 1/2 cup dark chocolate, finely chopped
- 1/2 cup almonds, toasted
- 3 cloves garlic
- 1/2 onion, chopped
- 1 tsp ground cinnamon
- 1/2 tsp ground cloves
- 1/2 tsp ground cumin
- 1/2 tsp ground coriander
- 1/2 tsp dried thyme
- 1/2 tsp dried oregano
- 4 cups chicken or vegetable broth
- 2 tbsp vegetable oil
- Salt to taste

Instructions

1. Remove seeds and stems from ancho and pasilla chilies. Toast until fragrant, then soak in hot water until soft.

2. In a blender, combine soaked chilies, maple syrup, dark chocolate, almonds, garlic, onion, and spices. Blend into a smooth paste.

3. Heat vegetable oil in a pot. Add the paste and cook over medium heat until it thickens.

4. Pour in chicken or vegetable broth. Simmer for 20-30 minutes, allowing the flavors to meld.

5. Season with salt to taste.

6. Serve or save to your preference and safety instructions.

Pumpkin Mole Chili

This Pumpkin Mole Chili is a culinary journey that marries the robust traditions of mole with the comforting familiarity of North American chili. By infusing the classic flavors of ancho chilies, cinnamon, and cloves into a velvety pumpkin puree, we've created a unique mole base that resonates with both depth and warmth.

The addition of unsweetened cocoa powder elevates the richness, echoing the traditional mole complexity. Intertwining this with ground pork or beef and hearty black beans transforms it into a North American chili, fusing diverse culinary worlds. This recipe pays homage to mole's essence while expanding its horizons, presenting a delightful balance of sweet and savory notes. With a nod to tradition and an embrace of innovation, this Pumpkin Mole Chili invites a cross-cultural celebration, a harmonious convergence of flavors that transcends culinary boundaries. Creating the White Bean Chocolate Cincinnati

Ingredients

- 2 tablespoons vegetable oil
- 1 medium onion, finely chopped
- 3 cloves garlic, minced
- 2 dried ancho chilies, deseeded and rehydrated
- 1 teaspoon ground cinnamon
- 1/2 teaspoon ground cloves
- 1 can (15 oz) pumpkin puree
- 1/4 cup unsweetened cocoa powder
- 1 cup vegetable broth
- 1 pound ground pork or beef
- 1 can (15 oz) black beans, drained and rinsed
- Salt and pepper to taste
- Garnish: pumpkin seeds, chopped fresh cilantro, lime wedges

Instructions

1. In a pan, heat vegetable oil over medium heat. Sauté chopped onions until translucent, then add minced garlic and sauté for another minute.

2. Blend re-hydrated ancho chilies with cinnamon, cloves, pumpkin puree, cocoa powder, and vegetable broth until smooth.

3. Brown ground pork or beef in the pan with the onion and garlic mixture.

4. Pour in the pumpkin mole sauce and add black beans. Stir well and bring to a simmer.

5. Season with salt and pepper to taste. Simmer for 20-25 minutes, allowing flavors to meld.

Cincinnati Chili

Chili was an exploration into blending diverse culinary traditions. Inspired by the essence of mole, we incorporated the richness of cocoa, coriander, and nutmeg into ground chicken, achieving a harmonious balance of sweet and savory notes. This innovative fusion not only respects the cherished traditions of North American chili but also pays homage to the complexity found in mole.

By embracing the sweet creaminess of white beans and the decadence of grated chocolate, we expanded the boundaries of Cincinnati Chili, offering a comforting yet sophisticated dish. The subtle warmth of coriander and nutmeg echoes the spices found in mole, creating a cross-cultural celebration that transcends culinary boundaries. In each spoonful, savor the union of tradition and innovation, making this White Bean Chocolate Cincinnati Chili a delightful journey into the artistry of flavor.

Ingredients

- 2 tablespoons olive oil
- 1 pound ground chicken
- 2 teaspoons cocoa powder
- 1 teaspoon ground coriander
- 1/2 teaspoon ground nutmeg
- 1 onion, finely chopped
- 2 cans (15 oz each) white beans, drained and rinsed
- 1 can (14.5 oz) diced tomatoes
- 2 cups chicken broth
- Salt and pepper to taste
- Grated chocolate and fresh cilantro for garnish

Instructions

1. In a large pot, heat olive oil over medium heat. Add ground chicken and cook until browned.

2. Sprinkle cocoa powder, ground coriander, and nutmeg over the chicken. Stir to combine and let it cook for an additional minute.

3. Add chopped onion to the pot and sauté until softened.

4. Pour in drained white beans, diced tomatoes, and chicken broth. Stir well.

5. Bring the mixture to a simmer. Season with salt and pepper to taste.

6. Simmer the chili for 15-20 minutes, allowing the flavors to meld and the chili to thicken.

Texas-Style Chocolate Chili

The genesis of the Texas-Style Chocolate Chili unfolded as a tribute to the robust traditions of North American chili, intertwined with the sophisticated nuances of mole. By selecting premium cuts of beef, infusing them with an array of aromatic spices, and enriching the broth with brewed coffee and dark chocolate, we crafted a hearty chili that embodies the bold spirit of Texas cuisine.

Drawing inspiration from mole, the amalgamation of cumin, smoked paprika, and coriander mirrors the depth found in traditional mole blends. The addition of dark chocolate elevates the richness, creating a velvety texture that echoes the complexities of mole. In every spoonful, this chili transcends traditional boundaries, celebrating both the rugged authenticity of Texas chili and the refined allure of mole, offering a harmonious fusion that pays homage to diverse culinary legacies.

Ingredients

- 2 tablespoons vegetable oil
- 2 pounds beef chuck, diced
- 1 large onion, diced
- 4 cloves garlic, minced
- 2 tablespoons chili powder
- 1 tablespoon ground cumin
- 1 tablespoon smoked paprika
- 1 teaspoon dried oregano
- 1 teaspoon ground coriander
- 1/4 cup tomato paste
- 1 can (14.5 oz) crushed tomatoes
- 2 cups beef broth
- 1 cup brewed black coffee
- 1 oz dark chocolate (70% cocoa or higher), finely chopped
- 2 cans (15 oz each) kidney beans, drained and rinsed
- Salt and pepper to taste
- Optional toppings: shredded cheese, chopped green onions, sour cream

Instructions

1. In a large pot, heat vegetable oil over medium-high heat. Add diced beef and brown on all sides. Remove and set aside.

2. In the same pot, sauté diced onion until softened. Add minced garlic and cook for an additional minute.

3. Sprinkle chili powder, cumin, smoked paprika, dried oregano, and ground coriander over the onions. Stir to coat.

4. Add tomato paste and cook for 2 minutes, stirring constantly.

5. Return the browned beef to the pot. Pour in crushed tomatoes, beef broth, and brewed coffee. Stir well.

6. Bring the mixture to a simmer. Add the chopped chocolate and let it melt into the chili.

7. Add drained kidney beans and simmer for 1.5 to 2 hours until the beef is tender and the flavors meld.

Season with salt and pepper to taste.

Ancho Chocolate Chili

Creating our Ancho Chocolate Chili was a culinary journey that harmonized the timeless traditions of mole with the hearty essence of North American chili. Inspired by the depth of mole, we crafted a blend of ancho and chipotle chilies, dark chocolate, and a symphony of spices, infusing the dish with layers of complexity. The slow-cooked beef, aromatic onions, and rich tomato base pay homage to the heartiness of North American chili.

By incorporating the smokiness of chipotle, the warmth of ancho chilies, and the velvety richness of dark chocolate, we expanded the boundaries of flavor. This fusion resonates with both the soulful traditions of mole and the robust character of North American chili, offering a unique and full-flavored experience that bridges culinary traditions in every savory spoonful.

Ingredients

- 3 tablespoons vegetable oil
- 2 pounds beef chuck, cubed
- 2 large onions, finely chopped
- 6 cloves garlic, minced
- 4 dried ancho chilies, deseeded and rehydrated
- 2 chipotle chilies in adobo sauce
- 1/4 cup tomato paste
- 2 tablespoons ground cumin
- 1 tablespoon smoked paprika
- 1 tablespoon dried oregano
- 1 teaspoon ground coriander
- 1 teaspoon cinnamon
- 1 oz high-quality dark chocolate (70% cocoa or higher), finely chopped
- 1 can (14.5 oz) crushed tomatoes
- 3 cups beef broth
- 1 cup strong brewed coffee
- 2 cans (15 oz each) black beans, drained and rinsed
- Salt and pepper to taste
- Optional toppings: shredded cheese, sliced green onions, cilantro, sour cream

Instructions

1. Heat oil in a large pot. Brown beef cubes, then set aside.

2. Sauté onions until caramelized. Add minced garlic.

3. Blend ancho chilies, chipotle chilies, and tomato paste until smooth.

4. Add the chili paste to the pot and stir.

5. Return beef to the pot. Sprinkle with cumin, smoked paprika, oregano, coriander, and cinnamon.

6. Add chopped chocolate, crushed tomatoes, beef broth, and coffee. Stir until chocolate melts.

7. Simmer for 2-3 hours until beef is tender.

Pork Shoulder New Mexico Red Chili with Chocolate

Indulge in the rich tapestry of Southwestern flavors with our Pork Shoulder New Mexico Red Chili with Chocolate. This innovative recipe intertwines the storied traditions of New Mexican red chili with a touch of decadence, as dark chocolate gracefully melds into the slow-cooked, succulent pork shoulder. The result is a harmonious blend of smoky heat and velvety richness, showcasing the time-honored marriage of chili and chocolate.

Rooted in the heart of Southwestern cuisine, this dish pays homage to its origins while pushing culinary boundaries. With each bite, savor the nuanced layers that elevate the familiar, transforming a classic into a culinary journey that bridges tradition and innovation, creating a Pork Shoulder New Mexico Red Chili with Chocolate that transcends the ordinary.

Ingredients

- 3 tablespoons vegetable oil
- 2 pounds pork shoulder, diced
- 2 large onions, finely chopped
- 4 cloves garlic, minced
- 6 dried New Mexico red chilies, deseeded and rehydrated
- 2 chipotle chilies in adobo sauce
- 1/4 cup tomato paste
- 2 tablespoons ground cumin
- 1 tablespoon smoked paprika
- 1 teaspoon dried oregano
- 1 teaspoon ground coriander
- 1 oz high-quality dark chocolate (70% cocoa or higher), finely chopped
- 1 can (14.5 oz) diced tomatoes
- 3 cups beef broth
- 1 cup strong brewed coffee
- 1 sweet potato, peeled and diced
- 1/2 cup dried apricots, chopped
- Salt and pepper to taste
- Optional toppings: chopped green onions, toasted pumpkin seeds, lime wedges

Instructions

1. Heat vegetable oil in a pot. Brown pork until golden, then set aside.

2. Sauté onions until translucent, then add minced garlic.

3. Blend New Mexico red chilies, chipotle chilies, and tomato paste until smooth.

4. Add the chili paste to the pot. Stir in cumin, smoked paprika, oregano, and coriander.

5. Return pork to the pot. Add chocolate, diced tomatoes, beef broth, and brewed coffee.

6. Simmer and add sweet potato and apricots.

7. Simmer for 2 to 2.5 hours until pork is tender.

8. Season with salt and pepper.

Oaxacan Black Bean and Chocolate Chili with Shrimp

In developing this Oaxacan Black Bean and Chocolate Chili with Shrimp, we drew inspiration from the rich culinary traditions of Oaxaca, Mexico. We aimed to create a harmonious fusion that respects the essence of traditional chili while pushing culinary boundaries. The marriage of black beans, ancho, and pasilla chilies, a hallmark of Oaxacan cuisine, adds depth and complexity. The inclusion of high-quality dark chocolate, paying homage to Oaxaca's famed mole sauces, introduces a velvety richness and subtle sweetness.

This recipe expands on the North American chili tradition by incorporating distinctive Oaxacan elements. The complexity of flavors, derived from the blend of chilies and chocolate, provides a unique taste experience. The addition of shrimp elevates the dish, introducing a seafood twist that's both innovative and delicious. By carefully balancing traditional roots with inventive elements, this recipe reflects a culinary journey that honors the past while embracing the evolution of flavors in contemporary cuisine.

Ingredients

- 2 tablespoons vegetable oil
- 1 large onion, finely chopped
- 4 cloves garlic, minced
- 2 dried ancho chilies, deseeded and rehydrated
- 2 dried pasilla chilies, deseeded and rehydrated
- 1 lb large shrimp, peeled and deveined
- 2 cans (15 oz each) black beans, drained and rinsed
- 1 can (14.5 oz) diced tomatoes
- 1 teaspoon ground cumin
- 1 teaspoon smoked paprika
- 1 teaspoon dried oregano
- 1/2 teaspoon ground coriander
- 1 oz high-quality dark chocolate (70% cocoa or higher), finely chopped
- 3 cups vegetable broth
- Salt and pepper to taste
- Optional toppings: crumbled queso fresco, chopped cilantro, lime wedges

Instructions

1. Heat vegetable oil in a large pot over medium heat. Sauté chopped onions until translucent, then add minced garlic and cook for 1 minute.

2. Blend rehydrated ancho chilies and pasilla chilies until smooth.

3. Add the chili paste to the pot, along with black beans, diced tomatoes, cumin, smoked paprika, dried oregano, and ground coriander.

4. Stir in the chopped dark chocolate and pour in the vegetable broth. Mix well.

5. Bring the chili to a simmer, then reduce heat and let it simmer for 20-30 minutes.

6. In the last 5 minutes of cooking, add the peeled and de-veined shrimp. Cook until the shrimp turn pink and opaque.

7. Season with salt and pepper to taste.

8. Add black beans and simmer for an additional 30 minutes.

9. Season with salt and pepper.

Cuban Black Bean, Ham, Pork and Chocolate Chili

Our Cuban Black Bean and Chocolate Chili with Ham and Pork presents a captivating blend of culinary influences and flavors, weaving a narrative that draws inspiration from the rich tapestry of Cuban gastronomy. Rooted in the tradition of hearty stews and aromatic spices, this chili stands out through its distinctive combination of black beans, savory ham, and succulent pork shoulder.

The inclusion of high-quality dark chocolate elevates the dish, marrying savory and sweet elements in a way that sets it apart from traditional chili recipes. This unique fusion offers a velvety richness and complexity that lingers on the palate. With each spoonful, the chili tells a story of culinary innovation, pushing boundaries while remaining true to the essence of Cuban cuisine. A celebration of bold flavors and thoughtful pairings, our Cuban-inspired chili stands as a compelling testament to the endless possibilities within the world of savory comfort foods.

Ingredients

- 2 tablespoons olive oil
- 1 large onion, diced
- 1 bell pepper, diced
- 3 cloves garlic, minced
- 1 teaspoon ground cumin
- 1 teaspoon dried oregano
- 1 teaspoon smoked paprika
- 2 cans (15 ounces each) black beans, drained and rinsed
- 1 can (14 ounces) diced tomatoes
- 1 cup diced ham
- 1 pound pork shoulder, cut into cubes
- 3 ounces high-quality dark chocolate, grated
- Salt and pepper to taste
- Fresh cilantro, for garnish
- Sour cream, for serving

Instructions

1. Heat olive oil in a large pot; sauté diced onions, bell peppers, and garlic until softened.

2. Add ground cumin, oregano, and smoked paprika; stir well. Incorporate black beans and diced tomatoes; let it simmer for a few minutes.

3. Add diced ham and cubed pork shoulder; stir to combine.

4. Grate dark chocolate into the pot; stir until melted.

5. Simmer over low heat for 30-40 minutes.

6. Season with salt and pepper to taste.

Super Simple Red Chili Mole

Our Super Simple Red Chili Mole Chili is a culinary symphony that harmonizes the soulful warmth of traditional chili with the exotic allure of Mexican mole. Born from a desire to innovate while respecting culinary heritage, this recipe transforms the ordinary into the extraordinary.

Diverging from conventional chili recipes, the infusion of dark chocolate adds an unexpected layer of complexity, creating a velvety texture and subtle sweetness. This unique blend transcends the boundaries of tradition, offering a distinctive flavor profile that captures the essence of mole without sacrificing simplicity. The chili stands out as a testament to the power of minimalism, proving that even with a handful of ingredients, one can craft a dish that is both unique and compelling. In this culinary creation, the meeting of chili and mole becomes a celebration of flavor, demonstrating that innovation can be found in the simplest of recipes.

Ingredients

- 1 tablespoon oil
- 1 onion, diced
- 3 cloves garlic, minced
- 2 tablespoons chili powder
- 1 teaspoon ground cumin
- 1 teaspoon smoked paprika
- 1 can (14 ounces) crushed tomatoes
- 2 cups chicken broth
- 1 pound ground beef or turkey, browned
- 3 ounces dark chocolate, grated
- Salt and pepper to taste
- Fresh cilantro, for garnish

Instructions

1. Heat oil in a pot; sauté diced onions and minced garlic until softened.

2. Add chili powder, cumin, and smoked paprika; stir to coat the aromatics.

3. Pour in crushed tomatoes and chicken broth; bring to a simmer.

4. Add browned ground beef or turkey, stirring to break it apart.

5. Grate dark chocolate into the pot, stirring until melted and incorporated.

6. Let the chili simmer for 15-20 minutes to meld flavors.

7. Season with salt and pepper to taste.

Aztec-Inspired Chocolate Chili

Our Aztec-Inspired Chocolate Chili stands as a culinary tapestry, weaving the rich tapestry of ancient Aztec flavors into a contemporary dish. What sets this chili apart is its meticulous blend of traditional spices — chili powder, cumin, and smoked paprika — with an infusion of distinctive Aztec elements like cinnamon, cayenne pepper, coriander, and cloves. This carefully curated spice medley offers a multi-layered heat, providing a sensory journey through time and culture.

The *pièce de résistance* is the addition of high-quality dark chocolate, a nod to the Aztecs' reverence for cacao. This luxurious ingredient not only enriches the texture but also imparts a bittersweet depth, creating a symphony of flavors that transcends the ordinary. Our Aztec-inspired creation is a celebration of ancient culinary wisdom, a dish that transports the palate to a realm where history and innovation coalesce in every savory spoonful.

Ingredients

- 1 tablespoon vegetable oil
- 1 onion, finely chopped
- 3 cloves garlic, minced
- 1 pound ground beef or turkey
- 2 cans (15 ounces each) black beans, drained and rinsed
- 1 can (14 ounces) diced tomatoes
- 2 tablespoons tomato paste
- 2 teaspoons chili powder
- 1 teaspoon ground cumin
- 1 teaspoon smoked paprika
- 1/2 teaspoon cinnamon
- 1/4 teaspoon cayenne pepper
- 1/4 teaspoon ground coriander
- 1/4 teaspoon ground cloves
- 3 ounces high-quality dark chocolate, chopped
- Salt and pepper to taste
- Fresh cilantro, for garnish
- Sour cream, for serving

Instructions

1. Heat oil in a pot; sauté onions and garlic until softened.

2. Add ground meat; brown and break apart with a spoon.

3. Incorporate black beans, diced tomatoes, and tomato paste; stir well.
Season with chili powder, cumin, smoked paprika, cinnamon, cayenne pepper, coriander, and cloves.

4. Add chopped dark chocolate; stir until melted and combined.

5. Simmer over low heat for 20-30 minutes to meld flavors.

6. Season with salt and pepper to taste.

Spicy Dark Chocolate Turkey & Cactus Chili

With our Spicy Dark Chocolate Turkey Chili with Cactus, we embark on a culinary journey that marries the lean essence of turkey with the distinct flavor and texture of cactus. This innovative fusion is a celebration of boldness and creativity in the kitchen. What sets this chili apart is the infusion of spicy dark chocolate, a masterstroke that introduces an enticing heat, making every bite an adventure for the senses. Adjust the spice levels according to your liking and savor the delightful interplay of flavors and textures. With a hearty base of turkey, succulent cactus, and the captivating allure of spicy dark chocolate, this chili invites you to explore the boundaries of traditional recipes, creating a uniquely satisfying and memorable dining experience.

Nopales, the flat stems of the prickly pear cactus, bring a mild, tangy flavor and crisp texture to the Spicy Dark Chocolate Turkey Chili. Their subtle citrus notes and unique ability to enhance surrounding flavors make them a refreshing addition that complements the hearty turkey and bold spicy chocolate, creating a harmonious and distinctive fusion.

Ingredients

- 1 tablespoon vegetable oil
- 1 onion, finely chopped
- 3 cloves garlic, minced
- 1 pound ground turkey
- 1 cup diced cactus (nopales), cleaned and cooked
- 2 cans (15 ounces each) kidney beans, drained and rinsed
- 1 can (14 ounces) diced tomatoes
- 2 tablespoons tomato paste
- 2 teaspoons chili powder
- 1 teaspoon ground cumin
- 1 teaspoon smoked paprika
- 1/2 teaspoon cayenne pepper
- 1/4 teaspoon cinnamon
- 1/4 teaspoon allspice
- 3 ounces spicy dark chocolate, chopped
- Salt and pepper to taste
- Fresh cilantro, for garnish
- Sliced avocado, for serving

Instructions

1. Heat oil in a pot; sauté onions and garlic until softened.

2. Add ground turkey; brown and break apart with a spoon.

3. Incorporate diced cactus, kidney beans, diced tomatoes, and tomato paste; stir well.

4. Season with chili powder, cumin, smoked paprika, cayenne pepper, cinnamon, and allspice.

5. Add chopped spicy dark chocolate; stir until melted and combined.

6. Simmer over low heat for 20-30 minutes to meld flavors.

7. Season with salt and pepper to taste. Garnish with fresh cilantro and serve with sliced avocado.

White Bean and Chocolate Chicken Chili

In crafting this culinary masterpiece, our White Bean and Chocolate Chicken Chili seamlessly intertwines the opulence of high-quality white chocolate with the robust flavors of tender chicken and wholesome white beans. The marriage of these minimal yet carefully selected ingredients produces a chili that is both luxurious and deeply gratifying.

The inherent sweetness of white chocolate plays a harmonious duet with the savory and smoky undertones, creating a symphony of flavors that dance on the palate. As you savor each spoonful, the delicate balance between sweetness and heartiness unfolds, inviting you to personalize the experience by adjusting the seasoning to your taste. This distinctive and indulgent twist on a classic dish transcends expectations, offering a culinary journey where simplicity meets sophistication, and every bite is a celebration of refined taste.

Ingredients

- 1 tablespoon olive oil
- 1 onion, diced
- 3 cloves garlic, minced
- 1 pound ground chicken
- 2 cans (15 ounces each) white beans, drained and rinsed
- 1 can (14 ounces) diced tomatoes
- 2 cups chicken broth
- 2 tablespoons tomato paste
- 2 teaspoons ground cumin
- 1 teaspoon chili powder
- 1/2 teaspoon smoked paprika
- 3 ounces high-quality white chocolate, chopped
- Salt and pepper to taste
- Fresh cilantro, for garnish
- Lime wedges, for serving

Instructions

1. Heat olive oil in a pot; sauté onions and garlic until softened.

2. Add ground chicken; cook until browned and crumbly.

3. Incorporate white beans, diced tomatoes, chicken broth, and tomato paste; stir well.

4. Season with cumin, chili powder, and smoked paprika.

5. Add chopped white chocolate; stir until melted and combined.

6. Simmer over low heat for 20-30 minutes to meld flavors.

7. Season with salt and pepper to taste.

8. Garnish with fresh cilantro and serve with sliced avocado.

Cherry Chocolate Chipotle Chili

Embark on a culinary odyssey with our bold, boozy, and minimal Cherry Chocolate Chipotle Chili, where the luscious richness of dark chocolate intertwines with the smoky allure of chipotle and the subtle sweetness of cherries. Elevating this flavor symphony is a splash of bourbon, infusing the chili with a spirited kick that adds depth and complexity. The result is a unique and satisfying chili that effortlessly marries bold, complementary flavors without overwhelming the senses.

The simplicity of this recipe ensures a hassle-free preparation, allowing the distinct character of each ingredient to shine through. Whether you prefer a gentle warmth or a fiery kick, this chili invites you to tailor the heat to your liking, delivering a delightful complexity that makes every spoonful a memorable journey through layers of taste and texture.

Ingredients

- 1 tablespoon olive oil
- 1 onion, finely chopped
- 3 cloves garlic, minced
- 1 pound ground beef
- 1 can (15 ounces) black beans, drained and rinsed
- 1 can (14 ounces) diced tomatoes
- 1 cup frozen cherries, pitted
- 2 cups beef broth
- 2 tablespoons tomato paste
- 2 teaspoons ground chipotle powder
- 3 ounces dark chocolate, finely chopped
- 1/4 cup bourbon or whiskey
- Salt and pepper to taste
- Fresh cilantro, for garnish
- Jalapeño slices, for extra heat (optional)

Instructions

1. Heat olive oil in a pot; sauté onions and garlic until fragrant.

2. Add ground beef; cook until browned and crumbly.

3. Incorporate black beans, diced tomatoes, cherries, beef broth, and tomato paste; stir well.

4. Season with ground chipotle powder. Add chopped dark chocolate and bourbon; stir until chocolate is melted.

5.Simmer over low heat for 20-30 minutes to meld flavors.

6. Season with salt and pepper to taste.

7. Garnish with fresh cilantro and, if desired, jalapeño slices for an extra kick.

Mango Habanero Chocolate Chili

Worked on as a culinary ode to balance, our simplified and lower heat version of Mango Habanero Chocolate Chili seamlessly unites contrasting elements for a milder, yet equally flavorful experience. Delighting the palate with the natural sweetness of mango, this chili embraces a subtle kick from the habanero pepper, inviting harmony in every spoonful. Inspired by the rich tapestry of chili history, where diverse ingredients converge, this recipe pays homage to the evolution of chili as a versatile dish. As the dark chocolate melts into the concoction, it adds a touch of indulgence and depth, enhancing the overall sensory journey. This rendition stands testament to the timeless appeal of chili, where innovation and tradition coalesce to create a dish that transcends heat levels and resonates with both culinary enthusiasts and those seeking a gentler introduction to the world of spicy delights.

Ingredients

- 1 tablespoon olive oil
- 1 onion, diced
- 3 cloves garlic, minced
- 1 pound ground turkey
- 1 can (15 ounces) black beans, drained and rinsed
- 1 can (14 ounces) diced tomatoes
- 1 cup frozen mango chunks
- 2 cups chicken broth
- 2 tablespoons tomato paste
- 1 teaspoon ground cumin
- 1 teaspoon smoked paprika
- 3 ounces dark chocolate, finely chopped
- 1 habanero pepper, seeds removed and finely chopped
- Salt and pepper to taste
- Fresh cilantro, for garnish
- Lime wedges, for serving

Instructions

1. Heat olive oil in a pot; sauté onions and garlic until softened.

2. Add ground turkey; cook until browned and cooked through. Incorporate black beans, diced tomatoes, mango chunks, chicken broth, and tomato paste; stir well. Season with ground cumin and smoked paprika.

3. Add chopped dark chocolate and habanero pepper; stir until chocolate is melted.

4. Simmer over low heat for 20-30 minutes to meld flavors.

5. Season with salt and pepper to taste. Garnish with fresh cilantro and serve with lime wedges.

Coffee Stout Chocolate Chili

In this culinary symphony, the richness of dark chocolate intertwines seamlessly with the boldness of coffee stout beer, creating a nuanced and inviting flavor profile. The brewed coffee adds a sophisticated layer, enhancing the overall complexity of the chili. This recipe is an ode to the art of culinary craftsmanship, where each ingredient plays a vital role in delivering a mild yet captivating chili experience. It beckons you to embrace the comforting warmth and rich depth present in every bowl, allowing you to tailor the seasoning to suit your unique palate. Whether enjoyed on a cozy evening or shared with loved ones, this mild and multi-layered Coffee Stout Chocolate Chili invites you on a sensory journey that celebrates the beauty of well-balanced flavors.

Distinguished by its harmonious blend of dark chocolate and coffee stout beer, our mild and multi-layered Coffee Stout Chocolate Chili offers a nuanced alternative to traditional chili recipes. Unlike its spicier counterparts, this recipe prioritizes a perfect balance of flavors, allowing the richness of dark chocolate and the robustness of coffee stout beer to take center stage. The subtle complexity introduced by brewed coffee sets this chili apart, providing a distinctive and satisfying twist to a classic comfort dish.

Ingredients

- 1 tablespoon olive oil
- 1 onion, finely chopped
- 3 cloves garlic, minced
- 1 pound ground beef
- 1 can (15 ounces) kidney beans, drained and rinsed
- 1 can (14 ounces) crushed tomatoes
- 1 cup coffee stout beer
- 1/2 cup brewed coffee
- 2 tablespoons tomato paste
- 2 teaspoons chili powder
- 1 teaspoon ground cumin
- 3 ounces dark chocolate, finely chopped
- 1 tablespoon Worcestershire sauce
- Salt and pepper to taste
- Fresh cilantro, for garnish
- Sour cream, for serving

Instructions

1. Heat olive oil in a pot; sauté onions and garlic until softened.

2. Add ground beef; cook until browned and crumbly. Incorporate kidney beans, crushed tomatoes, coffee stout beer, brewed coffee, and tomato paste; stir well. Season with chili powder and ground cumin.

3. Add chopped dark chocolate and Worcestershire sauce; stir until chocolate is melted.

4. Simmer over low heat for 20-30 minutes to meld flavors.

5. Season with salt and pepper to taste.

6. Garnish with fresh cilantro and serve with a dollop of sour cream.

Smokey Bacon and Pumpkin Chili

The Smoky Bacon and Pumpkin Chili offers a harmonious blend of savory and smoky flavors with a touch of richness from the dark chocolate. The crispy bacon provides a salty and savory undertone, complemented by the earthiness of pumpkin and the subtle sweetness of the chocolate. The smoked paprika and cumin contribute a warm, aromatic quality, enhancing the overall depth of the dish. The white beans bring a hearty texture, while the diced tomatoes add a burst of freshness.

The chili's seasoning, including chili powder and dried oregano, strikes a perfect balance, allowing the individual components to shine. The finishing touch of melted dark chocolate ties the flavors together, creating a luscious and satisfying chili experience. This dish is a delightful medley of contrasting tastes, offering a comforting and savory journey for the palate.

Ingredients

- 6 slices of bacon, chopped
- 1 large onion, finely chopped
- 3 cloves garlic, minced
- 1 pound ground beef (or ground turkey for a leaner option)
- 1 can (15 oz) white beans, drained and rinsed
- 1 can (15 oz) pumpkin puree
- 1 can (14 oz) diced tomatoes, undrained
- 1 cup beef or vegetable broth
- 2 teaspoons smoked paprika
- 1 teaspoon ground cumin
- 1 teaspoon chili powder
- 1/2 teaspoon dried oregano
- Salt and black pepper to taste
- 4 oz dark chocolate, chopped
- Fresh cilantro, chopped (for garnish)
- Shredded cheese and sour cream (optional, for serving)

Instructions

1. Cook chopped bacon until crispy in a large pot, then set aside.
2. In the same pot with bacon grease, cook chopped onions until softened, then add minced garlic.
3. Add ground beef, cook until browned, and stir in smoked paprika, cumin, chili powder, dried oregano, salt, and black pepper.
4. Add white beans, pumpkin puree, diced tomatoes, and broth. Mix well.
5. Simmer for 15-20 minutes on low heat.
6. Stir in chopped dark chocolate until melted and fully combined.
7. Adjust seasoning to taste.
8. Serve hot, topped with chopped cilantro and crispy bacon.
Optional: add shredded cheese and sour cream.

Thai-Inspired Chocolate Coconut Chicken & Shrimp Chili

This Thai-Inspired Chocolate Coconut Chili draws inspiration from the vibrant and diverse culinary tapestry of Thailand. The addition of dried shrimp, a common ingredient in Thai cuisine, contributes a unique umami complexity, enhancing the overall flavor profile. The introduction of dark chocolate to this traditional Thai dish adds a rich and velvety dimension, creating an exciting fusion of Thai culinary heritage with a chocolatey twist.

In Thai cooking, the balance of sweet, savory, spicy, and umami flavors is paramount. The deep, complex notes of dark chocolate seamlessly complement the coconut milk, lemongrass, and red curry paste, elevating the dish to new heights. This innovative blend not only pays homage to Thai culinary traditions but also highlights the versatility of chocolate as a harmonizing element in global cuisines. The result is a captivating and indulgent Thai-inspired chili that captures the essence of both tradition and creativity.

Ingredients

- 1 tablespoon vegetable oil
- 2 stalks lemongrass, finely chopped
- 2 tablespoons red curry paste
- 1 pound ground chicken
- 1 can coconut milk
- 2 cups chicken broth
- 1/4 cup dark chocolate, chopped
- Handful of dried shrimp
- Salt and pepper to taste
- Fresh cilantro and lime for garnish

Instructions

1. Heat vegetable oil in a large pot over medium heat.

2. Sauté finely chopped lemongrass and red curry paste until fragrant.

3. Add ground chicken and cook until browned.

4. Pour in coconut milk and chicken broth, bringing the mixture to a simmer.
Stir in dark chocolate until melted and integrated.

5. Add dried shrimp for an extra umami kick.

6. Season with salt and pepper, adjusting spice levels to taste.

7. Simmer for 20-30 minutes to allow flavors to meld.

8. Serve hot, garnished with fresh cilantro and a squeeze of lime.

Ginger Chocolate Bison Chili

Combine robust game flavors with the zing of ginger in this Ginger Chocolate Bison Chili. The boldness of bison meat melds seamlessly with the warmth of fresh ginger, creating a chili that's rich in depth and complexity. The addition of dark chocolate enhances the overall experience, introducing a velvety richness and subtle sweetness to balance the spiciness. Adjust the heat level according to your preference and savor the fusion of gamey goodness and invigorating ginger in every hearty spoonful. This innovative recipe celebrates the adventurous side of chili-making, offering a unique and indulgent twist on a classic dish that's sure to delight the palate.

Using bison in chili imparts a unique and robust flavor profile, characterized by a slightly sweet and lean meat texture. Bison's natural richness complements the deep, savory notes of chili, offering a healthier alternative to traditional beef while contributing to a distinctive taste experience.

Ingredients

- 2 pounds bison meat, diced
- 2 tablespoons olive oil
- 1 large onion, chopped
- 4 cloves garlic, minced
- 2 tablespoons fresh ginger, finely chopped
- 1 can (28 ounces) crushed tomatoes
- 4 cups beef broth
- 4 ounces dark chocolate, diced
- 2 tablespoons chili powder
- 1 tablespoon ground cumin
- 1 teaspoon paprika
- Salt and pepper to taste
- Fresh cilantro or sour cream for garnish

Instructions

1. Heat olive oil in a large pot over medium heat.

2. Add diced bison meat and cook until browned.

3. Stir in chopped onions, garlic, and fresh ginger, sautéing until softened.
Incorporate crushed tomatoes, beef broth, and diced dark chocolate. Stir until chocolate melts.

4. Season with chili powder, cumin, paprika, salt, and pepper. Mix well.

5. Simmer over low heat for 30-40 minutes, allowing flavors to meld.

6. Adjust seasoning as needed.

7. Serve hot, garnished with fresh cilantro or a dollop of sour cream.

Caramelized Onion and Cocoa Chili

Caramelized Onion and Chocolate Chili is an exquisite fusion of slow-cooked caramelized onions and the sophisticated richness of chocolate, creating a chili that transcends the ordinary. This culinary masterpiece elevates traditional flavors by introducing a symphony of sweet, savory, and bitter notes. The nuanced use of coca, instead of conventional chocolate, adds a layer of complexity and depth, transforming the chili into a sophisticated indulgence.

The slow caramelization process enhances the natural sweetness of onions, harmonizing perfectly with the bittersweet undertones of coca. This chili is a celebration of culinary innovation, challenging expectations and inviting enthusiasts to savor a truly distinctive and memorable dish that blurs the lines between comfort food and gourmet artistry.

Ingredients

- 1 lb ground beef
- 2 large onions, thinly sliced
- 3 cloves garlic, minced
- 1 can (14 oz) diced tomatoes, undrained
- 1 can (14 oz) kidney beans, drained and rinsed
- 1 can (14 oz) black beans, drained and rinsed
- 1/4 cup tomato paste
- 1 cup beef broth
- 2 oz cocoa, finely chopped
- 2 tbsp chili powder
- 1 tsp cumin
- 1/2 tsp smoked paprika
- Salt and pepper to taste
- Olive oil for cooking

Instructions

1. In a large pot, heat olive oil over medium heat. Add sliced onions and cook until caramelized, about 15-20 minutes.

2. Add minced garlic and ground beef to the pot. Cook until the beef is browned, breaking it apart with a spoon as it cooks.

3. Stir in the diced tomatoes, kidney beans, black beans, tomato paste, and beef broth.

4. Add the chopped coca, chili powder, cumin, smoked paprika, salt, and pepper. Mix well to combine.

5. Bring the chili to a simmer and let it cook for at least 30 minutes to allow the flavors to meld.

Smoky Paprika Chocolate Chili with Game Meats

This Smoky Paprika Chocolate Chili with Game Meats has redefined the classic chili experience, introducing a harmonious blend of smoky richness and gamey depth. The inclusion of mixed game meats, such as venison, bison, and wild boar, imparts a unique flavor profile, elevating this dish to a new level of culinary sophistication.

The smoky essence from paprika, combined with the earthy notes of cumin and the subtle warmth of chili powder, creates a symphony of flavors. The addition of dark chocolate introduces a velvety complexity, perfectly complementing the hearty meats. This recipe not only pays homage to the timeless tradition of chili but also pushes culinary boundaries, making it a modern classic that captures the essence of bold innovation and indulgent comfort in every spoonful.

Ingredients

- 1 lb mixed game meats (venison, bison, wild boar), diced
- 2 tablespoons olive oil
- 2 large onions, finely chopped
- 4 cloves garlic, minced
- 2 tablespoons smoked paprika
- 1 teaspoon ground cumin
- 1 teaspoon dried oregano
- 1 teaspoon chili powder
- 1 teaspoon cocoa powder
- 1 cup dark chocolate, chopped
- 1 can (15 oz) diced tomatoes
- 1 can (15 oz) black beans, drained and rinsed
- 1 can (15 oz) kidney beans, drained and rinsed
- 1 cup beef or game broth
- Salt and black pepper to taste
- 1/4 cup gin (for Option 2)
- Fresh cilantro and sour cream for garnish

Instructions

1. In a large pot, heat olive oil over medium heat. Add onions and garlic; sauté until softened.

2. Add the mixed game meats to the pot, cooking until browned on all sides.

3. Stir in smoked paprika, ground cumin, dried oregano, chili powder, and cocoa powder. Mix well to coat the meat evenly.

4. Add chopped dark chocolate, diced tomatoes, black beans, kidney beans, and broth. Season with salt and black pepper.

5. Simmer the chili over low heat for 1.5 to 2 hours, allowing flavors to meld. Adjust seasoning as needed.

Chili Chocolate Beef Pie

This savory creation blends the richness of dark chocolate with the heat of chipotle peppers in a delectable chili beef pie. Originating from a fusion of Mexican and American influences, this recipe draws inspiration from traditional flavors. The process begins by browning ground beef with onions and garlic, creating a fragrant base. The addition of black beans, diced tomatoes, and a medley of spices such as ancho chili powder, smoked paprika, cumin, salt, and black pepper infuses a robust southwestern essence.

The surprise element comes with the integration of dark chocolate, elevating the dish with a velvety, bittersweet undertone. Encased in a golden-brown crust, this chili chocolate beef pie pays homage to diverse culinary roots, offering a symphony of flavors that tantalize the taste buds with every indulgent bite.

Ingredients

- 1 1/2 lbs ground beef
- 1 large onion, diced
- 4 cloves garlic, minced
- 1 can (15 oz) black beans, drained and rinsed
- 1 can (14 oz) diced tomatoes
- 2 chipotle peppers in adobo sauce, finely chopped
- 2 tablespoons ancho chili powder
- 1 tablespoon smoked paprika
- 1 teaspoon cumin
- Salt and black pepper to taste
- 1 cup dark chocolate chips or chopped dark chocolate
- 2 pre-made pie crusts (for top and bottom)

Instructions

1. Brown the ground beef in a large skillet over medium heat. Add diced onions and garlic, cooking until softened.

2. Stir in black beans, diced tomatoes, chipotle peppers, ancho chili powder, smoked paprika, cumin, salt, and black pepper. Simmer for 15-20 minutes.

3. Stir in dark chocolate until melted and well combined.

4.Line a pie dish with one pie crust, pour in the chili mixture, and cover with the second pie crust.

5. Bake according to the pie crust instructions or until the crust is golden brown.

Bacon and Chocolate Quiche

The Bacon and Chocolate Quiche represents a bold fusion of flavors, marrying the savory essence of crisp bacon with the sweet luxury of dark chocolate. Rooted in the adaptable tradition of French quiches, this modern creation introduces a novel interplay of tastes. The custard-like texture, heightened by the creamy Swiss cheese and a subtle hint of nutmeg, achieves a perfect equilibrium.

Ideal for brunch enthusiasts, dessert aficionados, and those intrigued by culinary experimentation, this quiche invites exploration beyond conventional boundaries. It stands as a testament to the dynamic nature of taste, providing a unique and unforgettable experience where the smokiness of bacon and the richness of chocolate converge. A conversation starter at gatherings, it caters to adventurous palates, making a lasting impression with its unexpected yet harmonious pairing.

Ingredients

- 1 pre-made pie crust (store-bought or homemade)
- 6 slices of bacon, cooked and crumbled
- 1 cup shredded Swiss cheese
- 4 large eggs
- 1 cup half-and-half
- 1/2 cup milk
- 1/2 cup dark chocolate chips
- Salt and black pepper to taste
- Pinch of nutmeg (optional)

Instructions

1. 1. Preheat your oven to 375°F (190°C).

2. If using a store-bought pie crust, follow the package instructions for pre-baking. If using homemade, pre-bake until lightly golden.

3. In a skillet, cook the bacon until crisp. Allow it to cool, then crumble it into small pieces.

4. Sprinkle the crumbled bacon evenly over the pre-baked pie crust. Add the shredded Swiss cheese on top.

5. In a bowl, whisk together the eggs, half-and-half, and milk. Season with salt, black pepper, and a pinch of nutmeg if desired.

6. Pour the egg mixture over the bacon and cheese in the pie crust.

7. Sprinkle dark chocolate chips evenly over the egg mixture. The combination of savory bacon and sweet chocolate creates a delicious contrast.

8. Bake in the preheated oven for 35-40 minutes or until the center is set, and the top is golden brown.

9. Allow the quiche to cool for a few minutes before slicing. Serve warm and enjoy the delightful combination of bacon and chocolate in each bite.

Thai-inspired Peanut and Chocolate Zucchini Pie

The Thai-inspired Peanut and Chocolate Zucchini Pie is a culinary journey into the harmonious fusion of Thai flavors and chocolate decadence. This innovative creation combines thinly sliced zucchinis, red bell peppers, and mushrooms, sautéed with a blend of Thai red curry paste, soy sauce, and rich peanut butter. The addition of dark chocolate chips imparts a luscious sweetness that perfectly complements the savory Thai-inspired filling. This pie represents a contemporary twist on traditional Thai cuisine, showcasing the versatility of chocolate in unexpected pairings. Ideal for those who appreciate adventurous and globally inspired dishes, this pie caters to a diverse palate, offering a delightful balance of spicy, savory, and sweet notes.

Perfect for gatherings or as a standout dessert option, this Thai-inspired creation is a testament to the exciting possibilities that arise when bold flavors come together in a familiar pie format.

Ingredients

- 1 pre-made pie crust
- 2 medium zucchinis, thinly sliced
- 1 red bell pepper, diced
- 1 cup mushrooms, sliced
- 1 onion, finely chopped
- 2 cloves garlic, minced
- 1/2 cup dark chocolate chips
- 1/4 cup creamy peanut butter
- 2 tablespoons Thai red curry paste
- 1 teaspoon soy sauce
- Salt and pepper to taste

Instructions

1. Preheat oven to 375°F (190°C). In a skillet, sauté onions and garlic until softened. Add zucchini, red bell pepper, and mushrooms. Cook until vegetables are tender.

2. Stir in Thai red curry paste, soy sauce, peanut butter, and dark chocolate chips. Mix until chocolate is melted and ingredients are well combined.

3. Pour the peanut-chocolate mixture into the pie crust.

4. Bake for 25-30 minutes or until the crust is golden brown.

Bison Cube Pie with Cocoa and Port Wine Gravy

The Bison Cube Pie with cocoa and port wine gravy is a savory masterpiece marrying the robust essence of bison with the decadent allure of cocoa-infused port wine gravy. This dish pays homage to the rich history of British savory pies, elevating the tradition with unexpected flavors. The cocoa imparts a subtle sweetness to the velvety gravy, complementing the tender bison cubes. The infusion of port wine adds a touch of luxury, while the pastry crust crowns the pie with a golden finish.

This creation appeals to those with a penchant for culinary adventure, appreciating the marriage of savory and sweet. Perfect for enthusiasts of traditional British fare seeking a contemporary twist, this Bison Cube Pie promises a memorable dining experience, blending history, innovation, and indulgence in every delectable bite.

Ingredients

- 2 pounds bison stew meat, cubed
- 2 tablespoons all-purpose flour
- 2 tablespoons vegetable oil
- 1 large onion, finely chopped
- 2 carrots, diced
- 2 celery stalks, diced
- 2 cloves garlic, minced
- 1 cup port wine
- 2 cups beef or bison broth
- 2 tablespoons tomato paste
- 2 tablespoons unsweetened cocoa powder
- 1 teaspoon dried thyme
- 1 teaspoon dried rosemary
- Salt and black pepper to taste

Instructions

1. Preheat your oven to 375°F (190°C).

2. In a bowl, toss bison cubes with flour until coated evenly.
3. Heat vegetable oil in a large oven-safe pot. Brown the bison cubes on all sides. Remove and set aside.

4. In the same pot, sauté onions, carrots, celery, and garlic until softened.

5. Pour in the port wine to deglaze the pot, scraping up any browned bits from the bottom.

6. Stir in tomato paste, cocoa powder, thyme, rosemary, salt, and black pepper. Pour in the broth, and return the browned bison cubes to the pot. Bring to a simmer.

7. Cover the pot and transfer it to the preheated oven. Bake for about 2 hours or until the bison is tender.

8. Roll out the puff pastry or pie crust and place it over the pot, sealing the edges. Cut a few slits on top for ventilation.

9. Bake for an additional 20-25 minutes or until the pastry is golden brown.

10. Let the pie cool slightly before serving. Slice and enjoy the rich and flavorful Bison Cube Pie with cocoa and port wine gravy.

Savory Chocolate-Peanut Butter 'Whoopie' Pies, an *Amuse-bouche*

The creation of these posh Savory Chocolate-Nut Butter Whoopie Pies ventures into a whimsical realm of culinary fusion. Inspired by a desire to blend sophistication with playfulness, this unique mash-up combines the richness of infused honey, the nutty elegance of almond or cashew butter, and the savory allure of chicken. Rooted in the evolution of gourmet tastes, this concoction defies culinary norms, marrying unexpected ingredients with a touch of absurdity. Tasting notes unveil a harmonious dance of flavors—nutty, earthy, and subtly sweet.

History meets innovation in this dish, embodying the contemporary spirit of gastronomic experimentation. Suited for those who relish culinary adventures, this creation appeals to the curious and daring, inviting them to experience a bite-sized marvel that transcends traditional boundaries. It's a playful indulgence for those seeking the extraordinary in their culinary journey.

Ingredients

For the Savory Filling:
- 1 cup cooked and shredded chicken breast
- 1/2 cup cashew butter
- 1/4 cup tamari sauce
- 2 tablespoons sesame oil
- 1 tablespoon wildflower honey
- 1 teaspoon minced garlic
- 1 teaspoon grated ginger
- Chopped green onions and sesame seeds for garnish

For the Chocolate-Peanut Butter Buns:
- 2 cups all-purpose flour
- 1/2 cup unsweetened cocoa powder
- 1 teaspoon baking powder
- 1/2 teaspoon baking soda
- 1/2 teaspoon salt
- 1/2 cup unsalted butter, softened
- 1 cup brown sugar, packed
- 2 large eggs
- 1 teaspoon vanilla extract
- 1 cup buttermilk-

Instructions

Prepare Chocolate-Peanut Butter Buns:
In a bowl, whisk together flour, cocoa powder, baking powder, baking soda, and salt. In another bowl, cream together butter and brown sugar. Add eggs and vanilla extract, then gradually mix in the dry ingredients alternating with buttermilk. Drop spoonfuls onto a baking sheet and bake until firm.

Create Savory Filling:
Mix shredded chicken with peanut butter, soy sauce, sesame oil, honey, minced garlic, and grated ginger. Adjust flavors to taste.

Assemble Savory Whoopie Pies:
Once the chocolate-peanut butter buns are cool, spread the savory chicken filling on the flat side of one bun and top with another to create a pie.

Garnish:
Garnish with chopped green onions and sesame seeds for an added savory touch.

Cocoa-infused Street Corn and Shrimp Empanadas

Empanadas, with roots tracing back to medieval Iberia, have evolved into a beloved culinary tradition across Latin America and beyond. Originating from the Spanish verb "empanar," meaning to wrap or coat in bread, these stuffed pastries showcase diverse cultural influences. Meanwhile, street corn, known as elote, reflects Mesoamerican origins, cherished for centuries for its simplicity and bold flavors.

In crafting Cocoa-infused Street Corn and Shrimp Empanadas, we weave together these historical threads. The cocoa-infused dough nods to the ancient Mesoamerican appreciation for cocoa, adding depth to the traditional empanada. By incorporating street corn, we celebrate its journey from humble beginnings to a street food sensation.

This fusion dish pays homage to the rich tapestry of Latin American culinary heritage, where empanadas and street corn converge with a modern twist. We aim to create a harmonious marriage of history and innovation, inviting enthusiasts to savor a delightful blend of traditional flavors elevated by a cocoa-infused twist.

Ingredients

For the Filling:
- 1 cup grilled corn kernels
- 1/2 pound cooked shrimp, chopped
- 1/4 cup mayonnaise
- 1 tablespoon lime juice
- 1 teaspoon smoked paprika
- Salt and pepper to taste

For the Cocoa-infused Dough:
- 2 cups all-purpose flour
- 1/4 cup unsweetened cocoa powder
- 1/2 cup unsalted butter, chilled and diced
- 1/2 cup cold water
- 1 teaspoon sugar
- Pinch of salt

For the Egg Wash:
- 1 egg, beaten

Instructions

For the Filling:
1. Mix grilled corn, chopped shrimp, mayonnaise, lime juice, smoked paprika, salt, and pepper in a bowl.

Cocoa-infused Dough:
1. In a food processor, blend flour, cocoa powder, butter, sugar, and salt until crumbly.
2. Gradually add cold water, pulsing until dough forms. Add more water if needed.
3. Transfer dough to a floured surface, lightly knead, and shape into a disc. Wrap in plastic and refrigerate for 30 minutes.

Assembly:
1. Preheat oven to 375°F (190°C); line a baking sheet with parchment paper.
2. Roll out chilled dough to 1/8 inch thickness.
3. Cut circles from the dough.
4. Spoon shrimp-corn filling onto each circle.
5. Fold dough over filling, press edges to seal, and crimp with a fork.
6. Place empanadas on the baking sheet.
7. Brush with beaten egg.
8. Bake for 15-20 minutes until golden.
9. Cool briefly before serving.

Citrusy Chocolate Asparagus Risotto

In this delightful Citrusy Chocolate Asparagus Risotto, the harmonious marriage of savory and sweet takes center stage. The recipe unfolds with the sautéing of asparagus in olive oil until tender, lending a fresh, vibrant element. The risotto preparation involves a symphony of flavors—onions and garlic infuse richness into Arborio rice, deglazed with white wine for depth. Gradually introducing warm broth ensures the creamy al dente texture characteristic of a perfect risotto.

The addition of orange zest and juice, along with the unexpected touch of cocoa powder, elevates the dish to a realm of contemporary sophistication. The marriage of citrus and chocolate creates a nuanced profile, while Parmesan and butter contribute to a velvety finish. Seasoned to perfection, the risotto is garnished with fresh parsley, offering a final flourish to this culinary masterpiece. This Citrusy Chocolate Asparagus Risotto promises a unique and memorable dining experience, blending tradition with inventive flair.

Ingredients

- 1 cup Arborio rice
- 1 bunch fresh asparagus, trimmed and chopped
- 1 small onion, finely diced
- 2 cloves garlic, minced
- 4 cups vegetable or chicken broth, kept warm
- 1/2 cup dry white wine
- 1/2 cup Parmesan cheese, grated
- 2 tablespoons unsalted butter
- 2 tablespoons olive oil
- Zest of 1 orange
- Juice of 1/2 orange
- 1 tablespoon cocoa powder
- Salt and black pepper to taste
- Fresh parsley, chopped (for garnish

Instructions

1. Heat 1 tablespoon olive oil in a pan. Sauté chopped asparagus until slightly tender. Set aside.

2. In a large pan, heat remaining olive oil. Add diced onion, cook until translucent. Add minced garlic and Arborio rice. Stir until rice is coated with oil.

3. Pour in white wine, stir until mostly absorbed by the rice.

4. Begin adding warm broth, one ladle at a time. Stir frequently, let liquid absorb before adding more. Continue until rice is creamy and al dente.

5. Stir in orange zest, orange juice, cocoa powder, and sautéed asparagus. Mix well.

6. Remove from heat. Add grated Parmesan and butter. Stir until creamy.

7. Season with salt and black pepper to taste. Garnish with fresh chopped parsley.

8. Spoon Citrusy Chocolate Asparagus Risotto onto plates. Optionally, sprinkle extra Parmesan on top.

Blue Cheese and Fig Chocolate Risotto

This Blue Cheese and Fig Chocolate Risotto embodies a contemporary fusion of flavors that marries tradition with innovative culinary expression. Rooted in the rich history of risotto, a classic Italian dish, this recipe takes a bold step by incorporating unconventional yet complementary elements. The warmth of chicken or vegetable broth serves as a canvas for the aromatic dance of sautéed onions, garlic, and the distinctive flavor of Arborio rice.

The addition of white wine introduces depth, while the infusion of crumbled blue cheese, chopped dried figs, and cocoa powder elevates this dish to a realm of sophisticated indulgence. The buttery finish adds a velvety texture, creating a harmonious blend of savory and sweet. This risotto, garnished with fresh thyme, offers a versatile dining experience—whether served as an elegant side dish or taking center stage as a gourmet main course, it promises to captivate palates with its intriguing and delectable profile.

Ingredients

- 1 cup Arborio rice
- 4 cups chicken or vegetable broth, kept warm
- 1/2 cup dry white wine
- 1 small onion, finely diced
- 2 cloves garlic, minced
- 1/2 cup crumbled blue cheese
- 1/2 cup dried figs, chopped
- 2 tablespoons unsalted butter
- 2 tablespoons olive oil
- 2 tablespoons cocoa powder
- Salt and black pepper to taste
- Fresh thyme leaves for garnish

Instructions

1. Warm chicken or vegetable broth in a saucepan on low heat.

2. In a large pan, heat olive oil. Add diced onion, cook until translucent. Add minced garlic and sauté until fragrant.

3. Add Arborio rice to the pan and toast for 1-2 minutes until edges become translucent.

4. Pour in white wine, stir until mostly absorbed by the rice.

5. Begin adding warm broth, one ladle at a time. Stir frequently, let liquid absorb before adding more. Continue until rice is creamy and al dente.

6. Stir in crumbled blue cheese, chopped dried figs, and cocoa powder. Mix until cheese is melted.

7. Remove from heat. Add unsalted butter and stir until creamy.

8. Season with salt and black pepper. Garnish with fresh thyme leaves.

9. Spoon Blue Cheese and Fig Chocolate Risotto onto plates. Optionally, top with additional blue cheese crumbles and a sprinkle of cocoa powder.

Pumpkin Sage Chocolate Risotto

The Pumpkin Sage Chocolate Risotto presents a contemporary symphony of flavors that reflects the inventive spirit of modern cuisine. This dish seamlessly melds traditional Italian risotto with unconventional elements, placing it at the forefront of culinary innovation. The warmth of roasted pumpkin and earthy sage harmonizes with the rich depth of cocoa, creating a comforting yet sophisticated indulgence. Its luxurious texture, enriched by Parmesan and butter, elevates the dining experience. As a culinary creation, this risotto captures the essence of autumn, offering a delightful play between sweet and savory notes.

A garnish of roasted pumpkin seeds adds a delightful crunch. In the repertoire of the modern chef, this recipe stands as a testament to the fusion of classic techniques with avant-garde creativity, appealing to discerning palates seeking both tradition and innovation on the plate.

Ingredients

- 1 cup Arborio rice
- 1/2 cup dry white wine
- 4 cups vegetable or chicken broth, kept warm
- 1 cup canned pumpkin puree
- 1/2 cup Parmesan cheese, grated
- 2 tablespoons unsalted butter
- 2 tablespoons olive oil
- 1 small onion, finely diced
- 2 cloves garlic, minced
- 2 tablespoons cocoa powder
- 1 tablespoon fresh sage, finely chopped
- Salt and black pepper to taste
- Roasted pumpkin seeds for garnish

Instructions

1. Warm the vegetable or chicken broth in a saucepan and keep it on low heat.

2. In a large pan, heat olive oil. Add diced onion and cook until translucent. Add minced garlic and sauté until fragrant.

3. Add Arborio rice to the pan and toast for 1-2 minutes until the edges become translucent.

4. Pour in the white wine and stir until it's mostly absorbed by the rice.

5. Stir in the canned pumpkin puree and chopped fresh sage. Mix well.

6. Begin adding the warm broth, one ladle at a time. Stir frequently and allow the liquid to be absorbed before adding more. Continue until the rice is creamy and al dente.

7. Stir in cocoa powder and grated Parmesan cheese. Mix until well combined.

8. Remove from heat. Add unsalted butter and stir until creamy.

9. Season with salt and black pepper to taste. Garnish with roasted pumpkin seeds.

10. Spoon Pumpkin Sage Chocolate Risotto onto plates. Optionally, top with additional Parmesan and a sprinkle of cocoa powder.

Lavender Honey Chocolate Risotto

This Lavender Honey Chocolate Risotto is a captivating exploration of sophisticated flavors, seamlessly blending floral notes with rich indulgence. The process begins with a lavender-infused milk, creating a fragrant base that elevates the entire dish. Diced onions sautéed to translucency set the stage for the Arborio rice, toasted to perfection. The risotto undergoes a gradual transformation as it absorbs white wine, followed by the creamy infusion of lavender-kissed milk. The addition of honey and cocoa introduces layers of sweetness and depth, while finely chopped dark chocolate, butter, and vanilla extract meld into a velvety symphony. A pinch of salt balances the ensemble, and optional edible lavender flowers provide a visual and aromatic flourish.

This unique creation is served with a touch of extravagance—dark chocolate shavings or a honey drizzle—a testament to the culinary artistry that seeks to delight the senses.

Ingredients

- 1 cup Arborio rice
- 1/2 cup dry white wine
- 4 cups milk (whole or plant-based)
- 1/4 cup honey
- 2 tablespoons dried culinary lavender
- 3 tablespoons cocoa powder
- 1/2 cup dark chocolate, finely chopped
- 2 tablespoons unsalted butter
- 2 tablespoons olive oil
- 1 teaspoon vanilla extract
- A pinch of salt
- Edible lavender flowers for garnish (optional)

Instructions

1. 1. Heat the milk and dried lavender in a saucepan over low heat. Bring to a gentle simmer, turn off the heat, and let it steep for 10-15 minutes. Strain out the lavender.

2. Warm the lavender-infused milk and keep it on low heat.

3. In a large pan, heat olive oil. Add diced onion and cook until translucent.

4. Add Arborio rice to the pan and toast for 1-2 minutes until the edges become translucent.

5. Pour in the white wine and stir until it's mostly absorbed by the rice.

6. Begin adding the warm lavender-infused milk, one ladle at a time. Stir frequently and allow the liquid to be absorbed before adding more. Continue until the rice is creamy and al dente.

7. Stir in honey and cocoa powder. Mix well.

8. Stir in finely chopped dark chocolate, unsalted butter, and vanilla extract. Mix until the chocolate is melted and the risotto is creamy.

9. Add a pinch of salt to taste. Garnish with edible lavender flowers if desired.

10. Spoon Lavender Honey Chocolate Risotto onto plates. .

Mexican Chocolate Spice Rub

This Mexican Chocolate Spice Rub combines high-quality unsweetened cocoa powder with a harmonious blend of ancho chili powder, cumin, coriander, smoked paprika, and other spices, creating a rich, smoky, and mildly spicy flavor profile. Its purpose is to elevate a wide range of dishes, adding depth and complexity to meats, vegetables, or even roasted nuts. The inclusion of finely ground coffee introduces a subtle, earthy undertone, enhancing the overall sensory experience.

This versatile spice rub innovatively marries traditional Mexican spices with the boldness of chocolate, offering a unique twist on conventional flavor profiles. The balanced combination of sweet (honey or maple syrup), savory (olive oil and garlic), and acidic (apple cider vinegar) in the wet mixture ensures a well-rounded taste. Stored conveniently in an airtight container, this spice rub stands as a go-to solution for infusing a touch of Mexican-inspired flair into everyday cooking, making it an indispensable addition to any kitchen seeking culinary creativity.

Ingredients

Dry Ingredients:

- 3 tbsp high-quality unsweetened cocoa powder
- 2 tbsp ancho chili powder
- 1 tbsp ground cumin
- 1 tbsp ground coriander
- 1 tbsp smoked paprika
- 1 tbsp ground cinnamon
- 1 tbsp finely ground coffee
- 1 tsp ground allspice
- 1 tsp ground nutmeg
- 1 tsp dried oregano
- 1 tsp dried thyme
- 1 tsp ground cloves
- 1 tsp ground black pepper
- 1 tsp sea salt
- 1/2 tsp cayenne pepper (adjust to taste)

Wet Ingredients:

- 2 tbsp olive oil
- 2 tbsp honey or maple syrup
- 2 tbsp apple cider vinegar
- 2 cloves garlic, minced

Instructions

1. Mix all the dry ingredients in a bowl: cocoa powder, ancho chili powder, cumin, coriander, smoked paprika, cinnamon, coffee, allspice, nutmeg, oregano, thyme, cloves, black pepper, sea salt, and cayenne pepper.. Ensure everything is well combined.

2. In another bowl, mix olive oil, honey or maple syrup, apple cider vinegar, and minced garlic.

3. Gradually pour the wet mixture into the dry mixture while stirring continuously, forming a thick paste.

4. Transfer the spice rub into a sealed container for storage.

5. Apply the mixture to meat or vegetables before cooking, letting it sit for at least 2 hours to enhance the flavors.

Mayan Cocoa-Rub

This innovative Mayan Cocoa-Rub harmoniously blends contemporary culinary finesse with ancient flavors, paying homage to traditional Mayan recipes. By combining high-quality unsweetened cocoa powder, ancho chili, and an array of aromatic spices like annatto, cardamom, and Mexican oregano, this rub presents a nuanced depth reminiscent of the Mayan spice palette. Its innovation lies in seamlessly infusing modern gourmet elements into a historically rooted concoction, creating a bridge between past and present.

This rub serves as a versatile enhancer for poultry, specifically chicken thighs, offering a distinctive taste that transforms everyday meals into culinary experiences. Its utility extends beyond mere seasoning, acting as a conduit for storytelling through food, connecting contemporary kitchens to the rich tapestry of Mayan culinary heritage. In essence, this Mayan Cocoa-Rub is a testament to the timeless allure of traditional recipes, intelligently reinterpreted for today's discerning palate.

Ingredients

- 3 tablespoons high-quality unsweetened cocoa powder
- 2 teaspoons ground cinnamon
- 2 teaspoons ancho chili powder
- 1 teaspoon ground cumin
- 1 teaspoon smoked paprika
- 1 teaspoon ground coriander
- 1 teaspoon ground allspice
- 1 teaspoon ground annatto seeds (achiote)
- 1 teaspoon ground cloves
- 1 teaspoon ground cardamom
- 1 teaspoon ground nutmeg
- 1 teaspoon dried Mexican oregano
- 1 teaspoon garlic powder
- 1 teaspoon onion powder
- 1 teaspoon sea salt
- 1/2 teaspoon black pepper
- 1/2 teaspoon cayenne pepper

Instructions

1. In a bowl, meticulously combine the high-quality unsweetened cocoa powder, ground cinnamon, ancho chili powder, ground cumin, smoked paprika, ground coriander, ground allspice, ground annatto seeds, ground cloves, ground cardamom, ground nutmeg, dried Mexican oregano, garlic powder, onion powder, sea salt, black pepper, and cayenne pepper.

2. Ensure an even distribution of all the spices, creating a complex and aromatic rub.

3. This sophisticated rub is now ready to elevate your culinary creations. Pat it onto chicken thighs, allowing the rub to adhere, and marinate for a minimum of 2 hours for an intensified flavor profile.

Southwestern Chocolate Ancho Rub

The Southwestern Chocolate Ancho Rub stands apart with its unique fusion of bold flavors, distinctively differing from the previous Mayan Cocoa-Rub. While both incorporate cocoa, this recipe focuses on the robust essence of the American Southwest and Mexican cuisines. Ground ancho chili powder takes center stage, infusing a deep, smoky heat, complemented by the earthy warmth of cumin and the savory notes of garlic powder.

The Southwestern rub exudes a vibrant, savory profile, contrasting with the more intricate, spiced complexity of the Mayan counterpart. Additionally, the Southwestern version features smoked paprika, providing a subtle smokiness absent from the Mayan rub, further contributing to its distinctive character. This innovative blend captures the spirit of two culinary traditions, offering a versatile and dynamic flavor profile ideal for grilling, roasting, or enhancing a variety of dishes.

Ingredients

- 3 tbsp unsweetened cocoa powder
- 2 tbsp ground ancho chili powder
- 1 tbsp ground cumin
- 1 tbsp garlic powder
- 1 tbsp smoked paprika
- 1 tsp ground coriander
- 1 tsp ground cinnamon
- 1 tsp dried oregano
- 1 tsp onion powder
- 1 tsp ground black pepper
- 1 tsp sea salt
- 1/2 tsp cayenne pepper (adjust to taste)

Instructions

1. In a bowl, combine cocoa powder, ancho chili powder, cumin, garlic powder, smoked paprika, coriander, cinnamon, oregano, onion powder, black pepper, sea salt, and cayenne pepper.

2. Thoroughly mix the ingredients for a balanced flavor profile.

3, Apply generously to meats before grilling, roasting, or cooking, allowing a minimum of 1 hour for the flavors to meld.

Aztec-Inspired Cocoa Pork Rub

The Aztec-Inspired Cocoa Pork Rub is a sophisticated marriage of high-quality unsweetened cocoa powder, ancho chili, and an array of traditional Aztec spices, curated to elevate the flavor profile of pork dishes. Distinguishing itself from previous rubs, this blend emphasizes ancho chili, lending a smoky depth, while the inclusion of ground cloves, nutmeg, and Mexican oregano offers a nuanced complexity reminiscent of ancient Aztec culinary traditions. The distinctiveness of this rub lies in its multifaceted flavor profile, combining rich cocoa notes with the warmth of cinnamon and cumin, creating a sensory journey that transports the palate to the heart of Mexico's gastronomic history. As a versatile seasoning, this rub not only enhances the taste of pork but also encapsulates the essence of Aztec-inspired culinary innovation, making it a unique and evocative addition to the culinary repertoire.

Ingredients

- 3 tablespoons high-quality unsweetened cocoa powder
- 2 tablespoons ancho chili powder
- 1 tablespoon ground cinnamon
- 1 tablespoon ground cumin
- 1 tablespoon smoked paprika
- 1 tablespoon ground coriander
- 1 teaspoon ground allspice
- 1 teaspoon ground cloves
- 1 teaspoon ground nutmeg
- 1 teaspoon dried Mexican oregano
- 1 teaspoon dried thyme
- 1 teaspoon ground black pepper
- 1 teaspoon sea salt
- 1/2 teaspoon cayenne pepper (adjust to taste)

Instructions

1. In a bowl, combine the high-quality unsweetened cocoa powder, ancho chili powder, ground cinnamon, cumin, smoked paprika, ground coriander, ground allspice, ground cloves, ground nutmeg, dried Mexican oregano, dried thyme, black pepper, sea salt, and cayenne pepper.

2. Ensure a thorough mixing of the ingredients to achieve a well-balanced and flavorful rub.

3. Generously rub the mixture onto pork before cooking, allowing it to marinate for at least 2 hours to intensify the taste.

Barbacoa Chocolate Espresso Rub

This *Barbacoa* Chocolate Espresso Rub offers a delightful fusion of simplicity and rich flavor, presenting a harmonious blend of cocoa, espresso, and Mexican-inspired spices. What sets it apart from other rubs is its approachable preparation, seamlessly combining distinct elements like ancho chili, smoked paprika, and a medley of spices. The rub caters to various palates, providing a nuanced taste that effortlessly transforms any *barbacoa*-style meat.

Barbacoa, a traditional Mexican cooking method, involves slow-cooking tougher and/or marbled meats, often beef or lamb, in an underground pit or a covered pot, resulting in tender, flavorful result. This rub enhances the experience by infusing *barbacoa*-style meats with the opulence of chocolate and espresso, complemented by the warmth of cumin and smokiness of paprika, creating a culinary masterpiece that embodies both simplicity and sophistication.

Ingredients

- 3 tablespoons high-quality unsweetened cocoa powder
- 2 tablespoons finely ground espresso beans
- 2 tablespoons ancho chili powder
- 1 tablespoon smoked paprika
- 1 tablespoon ground cumin
- 1 tablespoon ground coriander
- 1 tablespoon ground cinnamon
- 1 tablespoon dried Mexican oregano
- 1 tablespoon ground allspice
- 1 tablespoon ground cloves
- 1 tablespoon ground nutmeg
- 1 tablespoon ground cardamom
- 1 teaspoon ground turmeric
- 1 teaspoon ground black pepper
- 1 teaspoon sea salt
- 1/2 teaspoon cayenne pepper (adjust to taste)

Instructions

1. In a bowl, mix together all the ingredients.

2. Stir thoroughly to ensure an even blend, creating a simple yet flavorful rub.

3. Apply the rub generously to barbacoa-style meats, ensuring an even coating.

4. Let it marinate for at least 1 hour or, for enhanced flavor, leave it overnight in the refrigerator.

Cajun Chocolate Blackened Fish Coating

The Cajun Blackening Spice Mix has its roots in the vibrant culinary traditions of Louisiana, particularly Cajun cuisine, renowned for its bold flavors. This blend embodies the essence of Cajun spice, combining paprika, thyme, oregano, and a harmonious medley of peppers. The addition of cocoa in the Cajun Chocolate Blackened Fish Coating is a modern twist, marrying the rich essence of chocolate with traditional Cajun spices.

To use, generously coat fish fillets with this dynamic mix, pressing it into the flesh for optimal flavor. Pan-sear or grill the fish until a beautifully blackened crust forms, infusing the dish with smoky, savory, and subtly chocolatey notes. This versatile spice mix can also elevate chicken, shrimp, or vegetables, offering a simple yet sophisticated way to add depth and flair to your culinary creations.

Ingredients

Basic Cajun Blackening Spice Mix:

- 3 tablespoons paprika
- 1 tablespoon onion powder
- 1 tablespoon garlic powder
- 1 tablespoon dried thyme
- 1 tablespoon dried oregano
- 1 tablespoon cayenne pepper (adjust to taste)
- 1 tablespoon white pepper
- 1 tablespoon black pepper
- 1 tablespoon smoked paprika
- 1 tablespoon sea salt

For the Coating:

- 3 tablespoons Cajun blackening spice mix
- 1 tablespoon high-quality unsweetened cocoa powder
- 1 teaspoon smoked paprika
- 1 teaspoon ground coriander
- 1 teaspoon dried thyme
- 1 teaspoon onion powder
- 1 teaspoon garlic powder
- 1 teaspoon sea salt
- 1/2 teaspoon black pepper

Instructions

1. In a bowl, thoroughly mix together, by hand, all the ingredients for the Cajun Blackening Spice Mix together and reserve in an airtight container.

2. In a bowl, thoroughly mix together, by hand, all the ingredients for the Cajun Coating together and reserve in an airtight container.

Adobo Chocolate Chicken Rub

The Adobo Chocolate Chicken Rub intricately weaves Philippine influences into the blend, drawing inspiration from the renowned Filipino adobo technique. The inclusion of soy sauce, garlic, and Filipino cane vinegar pays homage to traditional adobo, infusing the rub with rich umami and tangy notes. Combined with high-quality unsweetened cocoa powder, cumin, and Mexican spices, it creates a harmonious fusion.

To use, generously coat chicken pieces, allowing the rub to marinate for an authentic flavor infusion. Grill or roast the chicken until succulent, with the robust flavors of adobo complemented by the smoky chocolate essence. This versatile rub enhances not only chicken but also pork or tofu, making it a perfect accompaniment to a diverse range of proteins, bringing the essence of Filipino-Mexican fusion to your dining table.

Ingredients

- 3 tablespoons high-quality unsweetened cocoa powder
- 2 tablespoons soy sauce
- 3 cloves garlic, minced
- 2 tablespoons vinegar (preferably Filipino cane vinegar)
- 1 tablespoon brown sugar
- 1 teaspoon ground cumin
- 1 teaspoon ground coriander
- 1 teaspoon smoked paprika
- 1 teaspoon ground annatto seeds (achuete)
- 1 teaspoon black pepper
- 1 teaspoon dried oregano
- 1 teaspoon dried thyme
- 1 teaspoon sea salt
- 1/2 teaspoon cinnamon
- 1/2 teaspoon cayenne pepper (adjust to taste)

Instructions

1. In a bowl, mix together all the ingredients.

2. Stir thoroughly to ensure an even blend, creating a simple yet flavorful rub.

3. Apply the rub generously to barbacoa-style meats, ensuring an even coating.

4. Let it marinate for at least 1 hour or, for enhanced flavor, leave it overnight in the refrigerator.

Easy Mole-Spiced Beef Rub

Incorporating the Easy Mole-Spiced Beef Rub introduces the rich, complex flavors of traditional mole to your culinary repertoire with utmost simplicity. By keeping the recipe straightforward, we capture the essence of mole spices in a user-friendly manner, ensuring accessibility without compromising authenticity. The blend of high-quality unsweetened cocoa powder, cumin, chili, and other spices mirrors the distinct profile of traditional mole, offering a taste journey reminiscent of Mexican culinary heritage.

This rub is an ideal choice for those seeking a quick yet authentic mole-inspired experience. Use it generously on beef cuts, allowing the robust flavors to infuse and elevate grilled, roasted, or cooked beef dishes effortlessly, transforming ordinary meals into a celebration of the vibrant and nuanced flavors found in classic mole recipes.

Ingredients

- 3 tablespoons high-quality unsweetened cocoa powder
- 2 tablespoons chili powder
- 1 tablespoon ground cumin
- 1 tablespoon smoked paprika
- 1 tablespoon dried oregano
- 1 teaspoon ground cinnamon
- 1 teaspoon garlic powder
- 1 teaspoon onion powder
- 1 teaspoon sea salt
- 1/2 teaspoon black pepper

Instructions

1. In a bowl, thoroughly mix together, by hand, all the ingredients and reserve in an airtight container.

Sweet & Easy Chocolate Chipotle Dry Rub

We're including this quick Chocolate Chipotle Dry Rub for its effortless appeal and versatile application in grilling and BBQ. Keeping it simple ensures accessibility while maintaining the authenticity of traditional rubs. This blend of unsweetened cocoa, chipotle, and a touch of brown or maple sugar captures the essence of classic BBQ flavors, balancing smokiness, sweetness, and savory notes. Its simplicity caters to both novice and seasoned cooks, making it an ideal choice for quick and crowd-pleasing meals.

Use it on chicken, pork, or beef to impart a delightful smoky-sweet profile, enhancing the natural flavors of the meat. This rub effortlessly elevates any grilling experience, ensuring a harmonious blend of familiar tastes and a hint of chocolate-infused sophistication to delight taste buds at any barbecue gathering.

Ingredients

- 3 tablespoons unsweetened cocoa powder
- 2 tablespoons chipotle powder
- 2 tablespoons brown sugar or maple sugar
- 1 tablespoon smoked paprika
- 1 tablespoon garlic powder
- 1 tablespoon onion powder
- 1 teaspoon ground cumin
- 1 teaspoon dried oregano
- 1 teaspoon sea salt
- 1/2 teaspoon black pepper

Instructions

1. In a bowl, mix together all the ingredients.

2. Stir thoroughly to ensure an even blend, creating a simple yet flavorful rub and reserve in an airtight container.

Tajín Chocolate Fruit Coating

In the radiant realm of culinary innovation, behold the Spicy Tajín Chocolate Fruit Coating – a divine symphony orchestrated by the gifted hands of flavor virtuosos. Picture the voluptuous elegance of dark chocolate, swirling harmoniously with the fiery spirit of Tajín, enticing your palate with a dance of chili, lime, and salt. As this ambrosial elixir delicately embraces succulent fruits, it unveils a revelation — a rhapsody of sweet and spicy ecstasy. The cayenne pepper, like a crescendo, weaves an intoxicating warmth, while honey and lime zest serenade the senses. Each bite, a celestial communion, transcends the ordinary, inviting you to savor the celestial union of flavors. In the grand tapestry of culinary marvels, this creation, a James Beard-worthy masterpiece, beckons you to experience the sublime marriage of spicy Tajín and decadent chocolate, leaving an indelible mark on the epicurean landscape.

Ingredients

- 1/2 cup Tajín seasoning (a Mexican seasoning blend with chili, lime, and salt)
- 1/4 cup high-quality dark chocolate, melted
- 2 tablespoons honey or agave syrup
- Zest of 1 lime
- 1/2 teaspoon cayenne pepper (adjust to taste)
- Assorted fruits (e.g., mango chunks, pineapple slices, strawberries)

Basic Tajín recipe:
- 1/4 cup ground chili powder (mild or hot, depending on your preference)
- 2 tablespoons ground dehydrated lime or citric acid
- 2 tablespoons sea salt or kosher salt
- 1 teaspoon dehydrated garlic powder
- 1 teaspoon dehydrated onion powder
- 1/2 teaspoon ground cayenne pepper (adjust to taste for heat)

Instructions

1. In a bowl, combine melted dark chocolate, Tajín seasoning, honey or agave syrup, lime zest, and cayenne pepper.

2. Mix the ingredients thoroughly to create a spicy and sweet Tajín Chocolate coating.

3. Dip each piece of fruit into the coating, ensuring an even and generous coverage.

4. Place the coated fruits on a parchment-lined tray.

5. Allow the coating to set by refrigerating the fruits for at least 30 minutes.

5 Chili Mocha Cocoa Rib Rub

Transport your taste buds on a historic journey with the Five-Chili Mocha Cocoa Rib Rub—a unique blend that beckons from centuries past to deliver an unparalleled culinary experience. This rub marries the richness of high-quality cocoa with the depth of five distinct chili varieties, embracing the smokiness of chipotle, the warmth of ancho, and the fiery allure of cayenne. Instant espresso elevates the profile, creating an engaging symphony of flavors that unfolds with each bite.

The inclusion of brown sugar, cinnamon, and cumin imparts a sweetness and spice that lingers on the palate, making it a historic and unforgettable rendezvous with flavor. As your ribs absorb this time-honored concoction, savor the fusion of ancient charm and contemporary allure, crafting a unique, engaging, and downright delicious chapter in your culinary repertoire.

Ingredients

- 3 tbsp high-quality unsweetened cocoa powder
- 2 tbsp instant espresso powder
- 1 tbsp ancho chili powder
- 1 tbsp chipotle chili powder
- 1 tbsp smoked paprika
- 1 tbsp cayenne pepper (adjust to taste)
- 1 tbsp brown sugar
- 1 tsp ground cinnamon
- 1 tsp ground cumin
- 1 tsp garlic powder
- 1 tsp onion powder
- 1 tsp sea salt
- 1/2 tsp black pepper

Instructions

1. In a bowl, mix together all the ingredients.

2. Stir thoroughly to ensure an even blend.

3. Apply the rub generously on ribs, ensuring even coverage.

4. Marinate the ribs for at least 2 hours, or overnight for optimal flavor.

Grapefruit Chocolate Chicken Rub for Caramelized Crust

This unique blend, enhanced by brown sugar's sweet embrace, promises a caramelized crust that elevates your dish to extraordinary heights. Picture succulent chicken, generously coated and marinated in this vibrant concoction, grilling to perfection. As the caramelized crust forms, anticipate a dance of zesty grapefruit, velvety chocolate, and a sweet undertone that harmonizes with every bite.

Unlike any other option, this rub beckons you with its perfect balance—capturing the essence of sweet, savory, and citrusy notes. Elevate your culinary experience, and let this Grapefruit Chocolate Chicken Rub be the reason your taste buds celebrate a symphony of irresistible flavors.

Ingredients

- 3 tablespoons high-quality unsweetened cocoa powder
- Zest of 1 grapefruit
- 2 tablespoons brown sugar or maple syrup
- 1 tablespoon smoked paprika
- 1 tablespoon garlic powder
- 1 tablespoon onion powder
- 1 teaspoon ground cumin
- 1 teaspoon dried thyme
- 1 teaspoon sea salt
- 1/2 teaspoon black pepper
- 1/2 teaspoon cayenne pepper (adjust to taste)
- 2 tablespoons olive oil

Instructions

1. Combine in a bowl: unsweetened cocoa powder, grapefruit zest, brown sugar or maple syrup, smoked paprika, garlic powder, onion powder, ground cumin, dried thyme, sea salt, black pepper, cayenne pepper, and olive oil.

2. Thoroughly mix the ingredients to form a vibrant Grapefruit Chocolate Chicken Rub with an extra sweet kick for caramelized crust.

3. Generously rub the mixture onto chicken pieces, ensuring an even coating.

4. Allow the chicken to marinate for a minimum of 30 minutes.

5. Grill, roast, or pan-sear the chicken until the rub creates a caramelized crust, enhancing the dish with a perfect blend of citrusy brightness, chocolate richness, and sweet caramelization.

Maple Bacon Chocolate Pork Rub

This tantalizing blend marries the rich, velvety notes of unsweetened cocoa powder with the savory crunch of finely chopped bacon, elevated by the sweetness of maple syrup and brown sugar. The ensemble is complemented by a medley of smoked paprika, cumin, garlic powder, and thyme, creating a harmonious balance of sweet and sour. As the pork absorbs this delectable concoction, each bite unveils a succulent, caramelized crust, encapsulating the essence of maple, bacon, and chocolate in perfect harmony.

Whether grilled, roasted, or smoked, this rub promises an unforgettable flavor journey, making it a must-try for those seeking an exquisite fusion of sweet, savory, and smoky notes in every delectable bite. Elevate your pork dishes with this unique and flavorful masterpiece.

Ingredients

- 3 tbsp unsweetened cocoa powder
- 2 tbsp finely chopped cooked bacon
- 3 tbsp maple syrup
- 1 tbsp brown sugar
- 1 tbsp smoked paprika
- 1 tbsp ground cumin
- 1 tsp garlic powder
- 1 tsp onion powder
- 1 tsp dried thyme
- 1 tsp sea salt
- 1/2 tsp black pepper
- 1/2 tsp cayenne pepper (adjust to taste)

Instructions

1. Combine cocoa powder, chopped bacon, maple syrup, brown sugar, smoked paprika, cumin, garlic powder, onion powder, thyme, sea salt, black pepper, and cayenne pepper in a bowl.

2. Thoroughly mix to craft the Sweet and Sour Maple Bacon Chocolate Pork Rub.

3. Generously apply the rub onto pork, ensuring an even coating.

4. Allow the pork to marinate for at least 30 minutes to absorb the sweet and sour essence.

Sesame Chocolate Soy Marinade

Crafted from soy sauce, dark sesame oil, high-quality cocoa powder, honey, and a symphony of spices, this recipe marries the bold flavors of cocoa and sesame with the umami depth of soy. While the marinade draws inspiration from Asian culinary traditions, the addition of cocoa adds a unique twist, creating a luscious and savory profile.

Marinating proteins for an extended period—whether chicken, beef, or tofu—allows the ingredients to meld, infusing every fiber with a complex depth. The soy sauce, when balanced with honey and other elements, ensures a nuanced, bold taste without overpowering saltiness. Embrace the journey of flavors, as the extended marination guarantees a protein masterpiece that's bold, rich, and distinctly memorable.

Ingredients

- 1/4 cup soy sauce
- 2 tablespoons dark sesame oil
- 3 tablespoons high-quality unsweetened cocoa powder
- 2 tablespoons honey
- 2 tablespoons rice vinegar
- 1 tablespoon grated fresh ginger
- 2 cloves garlic, minced
- 1 tablespoon toasted sesame seeds
- 1/2 teaspoon red pepper flakes (adjust to taste)
- Salt and black pepper to taste

Instructions

1. In a bowl, whisk together soy sauce, dark sesame oil, unsweetened cocoa powder, honey, rice vinegar, grated ginger, minced garlic, toasted sesame seeds, red pepper flakes, salt, and black pepper.

2. Ensure the marinade is well mixed, creating a bold fusion of flavors.

3. Coat your protein of choice (chicken, beef, tofu) with the marinade, ensuring an even distribution.

4. Allow the marination for at least 1 hour, or preferably overnight, in the refrigerator.

5. Grill, bake, or stir-fry the marinated protein for an exceptionally bold and flavorful dish,

Super Easy Honey Chipotle Chocolate Glaze

The Super Easy Honey Chipotle Chocolate Glaze presents a straightforward approach to culinary enhancement. Serving as a glossy coating applied post-cooking, a glaze, in the realm of culinary arts, aims to elevate both the visual appeal and flavor profile of a dish. This particular glaze, composed of honey, dark chocolate chips, and the nuanced heat of chipotle peppers' adobo sauce, delivers a balanced combination of sweetness, richness, and subtle spice. The distinct advantage of applying the glaze after cooking lies in the preservation of individual flavors. By doing so, the glaze maintains its integrity, allowing the eater to experience a delightful interplay of tastes without the risk of flavor dilution during the cooking process.

Versatile, this glaze enhances grilled meats, veggies, or desserts post-cooking. Deliberately applied, it transforms ordinary dishes with precision, creating culinary delights through a simple yet impactful technique.

Ingredients

- 1/4 cup honey
- 2 tablespoons dark chocolate chips
- 1 tablespoon adobo sauce from canned chipotle peppers (adjust to taste)
- Pinch of salt

Instructions

1. In a small saucepan, heat honey over low heat until it becomes runny.

Add dark chocolate chips to the honey and stir continuously until the chocolate is fully melted and incorporated.

Stir in adobo sauce, starting with a small amount and adjusting to your desired level of heat.

Add a pinch of salt to balance the sweetness and enhance flavors.

Remove from heat and let the glaze cool slightly before drizzling over your favorite dishes.

Cherry Cocoa Rub

The Cherry Cocoa Lamb Rub intertwines flavors inspired by culinary traditions and modern palates. Rooted in a love for unique taste combinations, this rub artfully marries the richness of unsweetened cocoa with the tangy essence of dried tart cherries. Historically, such fusions draw upon the depth of cocoa in traditional Mesoamerican dishes, converging with the sweet-tart undertones of cherries. Tasting notes unveil a symphony of flavors—cocoa's earthy warmth harmonizes with the bright tartness of cherries, creating a unique and enticing experience.

What sets this rub apart is its versatility. While designed for lamb, its charm extends to beef, pork, and poultry. The cocoa-cherry duo transforms grilled meats, adding a gourmet touch to roasts, and infusing complexity into pan-seared dishes. The Cherry Cocoa Lamb Rub stands as a testament to culinary evolution, blending historical inspirations with contemporary innovation for a uniquely delightful culinary journey.

Ingredients

- 2 tablespoons high-quality unsweetened cocoa powder
- 2 tablespoons dried tart cherries, finely chopped
- 1 tablespoon brown sugar
- 1 tablespoon ground cumin
- 1 tablespoon smoked paprika
- 1 teaspoon garlic powder
- 1 teaspoon onion powder
- 1 teaspoon dried thyme
- 1 teaspoon sea salt
- 1/2 teaspoon black pepper
- 2 tablespoons olive oil

Instructions

1. In a bowl, combine unsweetened cocoa powder, chopped dried tart cherries, brown sugar, cumin, smoked paprika, garlic powder, onion powder, dried thyme, sea salt, black pepper, and olive oil.

2. Mix the ingredients thoroughly to create a Cherry Cocoa Lamb Rub.

3. Rub the mixture generously onto lamb, beef, or chicken, ensuring an even coating.

4. Allow the protein to marinate for at least 30 minutes for the flavors to meld.

5. Grill, roast, or pan-sear the protein to perfection, unveiling a delightful fusion of cocoa richness and tart cherry sweetness

European Balsamic Chocolate Herb Coating

The European Balsamic Chocolate Herb Coating exudes a distinctly European flavor profile, combining rich unsweetened cocoa with a harmonious blend of Mediterranean herbs. This fusion captures the essence of European culinary traditions, where robust herbs like rosemary, thyme, oregano, basil, and parsley are often celebrated. The addition of balsamic vinegar elevates the coating with a touch of tangy sophistication commonly found in European cuisines.

This crowd-pleaser enhances a myriad of proteins, from succulent roasted chicken to grilled pork or seared beef. Its versatility allows it to complement vegetables, offering a gourmet touch to roasted root vegetables or grilled eggplant. The combination of cocoa richness and aromatic herbs creates a unique and delightful experience, making the European Balsamic Chocolate Herb Coating a surefire hit for gatherings and occasions, appealing to diverse palates with its savory, herbaceous, and subtly sweet notes.

Ingredients

- 3 tbsp unsweetened cocoa powder
- 2 tbsp balsamic vinegar
- 2 tbsp olive oil
- 1 tbsp dried rosemary, finely chopped
- 1 tbsp dried thyme
- 1 tbsp dried oregano
- 1 tbsp dried basil
- 1 tbsp dried parsley
- 2 cloves garlic, minced
- 1 tsp sea salt
- 1/2 tsp black pepper

Instructions

1. Combine cocoa powder, balsamic vinegar, olive oil, chopped dried rosemary, thyme, oregano, basil, parsley, minced garlic, sea salt, and black pepper in a bowl.

2. Mix the ingredients thoroughly for the European Balsamic Chocolate Herb Coating.

3. Generously coat your chosen protein with the herb-infused cocoa blend.

4. Allow the coating to marinate for at least 30 minutes to enhance the flavors.

5. Roast, grill, or pan-sear your protein, savoring the fusion of cocoa richness and aromatic European herbs.

Coconut Curry Chocolate Rub

This Coconut Curry Chocolate Rub delicately blends chocolate undertones with Thai green curry complexity. The minimal chocolate presence enriches without dominating, creating a light, intricate profile. Ingredients like cumin, coriander, and turmeric evoke Thai curry essence, while coconut adds gentle sweetness. Cocoa powder subtly deepens the rub's complexity.

Herbs like lemongrass, kaffir lime, and ginger balance the blend, enhancing its light, refreshing character. Tailored for those seeking sophistication, this rub elevates grilled chicken, seafood, or roasted veggies. It offers a nuanced flavor experience, subtly marrying coconut curry elegance with a hint of chocolate, promising a refined culinary journey.

Ingredients

- 2 tablespoons shredded coconut
- 1 tablespoon ground cumin
- 1 tablespoon ground coriander
- 1 tablespoon ground turmeric
- 1 tablespoon cocoa powder
- 1 teaspoon ground ginger
- 1 teaspoon ground lemongrass
- 1 teaspoon kaffir lime powder (or finely grated zest)
- 1/2 teaspoon ground black pepper
- 1/2 teaspoon sea salt

Instructions

1. In a bowl, mix shredded coconut, ground cumin, ground coriander, ground turmeric, cocoa powder, ground ginger, ground lemongrass, kaffir lime powder, black pepper, and sea salt.

2. Taste the mixture and adjust quantities for a balanced flavor. Add more salt if needed.

3. Rub the mixture onto your choice of protein or vegetables, ensuring even coverage.

4. Allow the rubbed items to marinate for at least 30 minutes. For a more intense flavor, marinate in the refrigerator for a few hours.

5. Grill, roast, or cook your marinated items as desired. The rub complements various cooking methods.

Ancient Arabic Cocoa Coffee Rub

This Ancient Arabic spice rub is a harmonious blend of cumin, coriander, cinnamon, ginger, turmeric, paprika, cloves, cardamom, nutmeg, black pepper, allspice, cocoa powder, sesame seeds, dried mint leaves, cayenne pepper, and sea salt. Its uniqueness lies in the convergence of rich, historical flavors that have characterized Arab cuisine for centuries. The warm and aromatic notes of cumin and cinnamon interplay with the earthiness of coriander, creating a nuanced base. Ginger and cloves add a hint of spice, while the exotic aroma of cardamom and nutmeg enhances the overall sensory experience.

The addition of cocoa powder imparts a subtle richness, elevating the rub to a distinctive level. Sesame seeds and dried mint contribute a delightful texture and freshness, creating a versatile spice blend that is ideal for marinating meats or enhancing the flavors of vegetables.

Ingredients

- 2 tbsp ground cumin
- 2 tbsp ground coriander
- 2 tbsp ground cinnamon
- 1 tbsp ground ginger
- 1 tbsp ground turmeric
- 1 tbsp ground paprika
- 1 tbsp ground cloves
- 1 tbsp ground cardamom
- 1 tbsp ground nutmeg
- 1 tbsp ground black pepper
- 1 tbsp ground allspice
- 1 tbsp cocoa powder
- 1 tbsp sesame seeds
- 1 tbsp dried mint leaves
- 1 tsp ground cayenne pepper
(adjust to taste for heat)
- 1 tsp sea salt

Instructions

1. Mix together cumin, coriander, cinnamon, ginger, turmeric, paprika, cloves, cardamom, nutmeg, black pepper, allspice, cocoa powder, sesame seeds, dried mint leaves, cayenne pepper, and sea salt.

2. Taste the mixture and adjust the quantities to achieve a balance that suits your taste preferences. If you like it spicier, add more cayenne pepper; if you prefer it milder, reduce the amount.

3. Rub the spice mixture onto your meat or vegetables, ensuring even coverage on all sides.

4. Allow the rubbed items to marinate for at least 30 minutes, or for a deeper flavor, refrigerate for a few hours or overnight.

5. Grill, roast, or cook your marinated items to perfection.

Smoked Almond Chocolate Pork Coating

The marriage of smoked almonds and dark chocolate introduces a distinctive richness, while nuanced spices like cinnamon, smoked paprika, and ground coffee add complexity. The gentle heat from chili powder or cayenne provides a subtle kick, and the incorporation of crushed crackers or panko breadcrumbs brings a satisfying crunch. Crafting this coating transforms a simple pork dish into a captivating exploration of taste and texture. Delve into the art of flavor layering, savoring each bite that marries savory, smoky, and subtly sweet notes.

The process becomes more than a mere recipe; it's an invitation to engage in the gratifying pursuit of culinary creativity, inviting appreciation for the unexpected harmony found in each mouthful.

Ingredients

- 1 cup smoked almonds
- 1/2 cup dark chocolate, finely grated
- 1 tsp ground cinnamon
- 1 tsp smoked paprika
- 1 tsp finely ground coffee
- 1/2 tsp chili powder or cayenne (adjust to taste)
- Salt and black pepper to taste
- 1 cup crushed crackers or panko breadcrumbs (for texture)

Instructions

1. In a food processor, blend smoked almonds, dark chocolate, cinnamon, smoked paprika, ground coffee, chili powder or cayenne, salt, and black pepper until coarsely mixed.

2. Add crushed crackers or panko breadcrumbs, pulsing briefly to maintain a textured consistency.

3. Pat pork dry and generously coat each piece with the almond-chocolate mixture, pressing it onto the meat for better adherence.

4. Bake or pan-fry until the pork reaches desired doneness and the coating forms a crispy crust.

5. Slice and serve the pork, savoring the unique blend of smoked almonds, dark chocolate, and spices. Enjoy this unconventional and flavorful pork coating!

Herb-Infused Chocolate Balsamic Glaze

Our Herb-Infused Chocolate Balsamic Glaze reflects a convergence of diverse flavors and techniques. Balsamic vinegar, with its roots in Italy dating back to the Middle Ages, serves as the base, marrying the richness of dark chocolate—a product of ancient Mesoamerican traditions. The infusion of thyme, rosemary, and peppercorns pays homage to the timeless use of herbs in European cuisines, adding depth and sophistication.

This versatile glaze embodies a balance of sweet and savory, heightened by the infusion process and the addition of honey or maple syrup, culminating in a velvety texture. Its uses are myriad: drizzled over grilled meats, roasted vegetables, or even desserts. This culinary innovation draws from historical influences, offering a contemporary twist that harmonizes the diverse culinary legacies of regions and eras.

Ingredients

-1 cup high-quality balsamic vinegar
-1/2 cup dark chocolate (70% cocoa or higher), finely chopped
-3 tablespoons honey or maple syrup
-1 teaspoon vanilla extract
-1 teaspoon dried thyme
-1 teaspoon dried rosemary
-1/2 teaspoon black peppercorns, freshly ground
-Pinch of sea salt

Instructions

1. Combine balsamic vinegar, thyme, rosemary, and peppercorns in a saucepan. Simmer for 10-15 minutes.

2. Strain infused vinegar and return to the saucepan.

3. Add finely chopped dark chocolate. Stir until melted.

4. Sweeten with honey/maple syrup, stir. Add vanilla extract.

5. Simmer over low heat until thickened (15-20 mins), stirring.

6. Season with a pinch of sea salt.

7. Cool before transferring to a jar. Glaze will thicken as it cools.

Hazelnut & Fig Chocolate Spread

This homemade Fig and Hazelnut Chocolate Spread combines the natural sweetness of figs with the richness of dark chocolate and the nuttiness of roasted hazelnuts. Blending these ingredients creates a velvety, indulgent spread with a delightful balance of flavors. The addition of honey or maple syrup enhances sweetness, while hazelnut oil ensures a smooth consistency.

Perfect for spreading on toast, crackers, or as a filling for pastries, this versatile treat elevates everyday snacks. For a gourmet touch, incorporate it into desserts like crepes, waffles, or layered parfaits. Use it as a filling for sandwich cookies or drizzle over ice cream for a decadent dessert. Whether as a simple spread or a creative addition to recipes, this Fig and Hazelnut Chocolate Spread adds a luxurious twist to any culinary creation.

Ingredients

- 1 cup dried figs, stems removed and roughly chopped
- 1 cup roasted hazelnuts
- 1/2 cup dark chocolate chips or chopped dark chocolate (70% cocoa or higher)
- 2 tablespoons cocoa powder
- 2-3 tablespoons honey or maple syrup (adjust to taste)
- 1 teaspoon vanilla extract
- Pinch of salt
- 2-3 tablespoons hazelnut oil or neutral oil (as needed for consistency)

Instructions

1. Blend figs, hazelnuts, dark chocolate, cocoa, honey, vanilla, and a pinch of salt.

2. Gradually add hazelnut oil until desired consistency.

3. Adjust sweetness to taste.

4. Blend until smooth.

5. Store in a jar in the fridge. Enjoy on toast or as a topping!

Bitter Strawberry Chocolate Marmalade

Our Herb-Infused Chocolate Balsamic Glaze reflects a convergence of diverse flavors and techniques. Balsamic vinegar, with its roots in Italy dating back to the Middle Ages, serves as the base, marrying the richness of dark chocolate—a product of ancient Mesoamerican traditions. The infusion of thyme, rosemary, and peppercorns pays homage to the timeless use of herbs in European cuisines, adding depth and sophistication.

This versatile glaze embodies a balance of sweet and savory, heightened by the infusion process and the addition of honey or maple syrup, culminating in a velvety texture. Its uses are myriad: drizzled over grilled meats, roasted vegetables, or even desserts. This culinary innovation draws from historical influences, offering a contemporary twist that harmonizes the diverse culinary legacies of regions and eras.

Ingredients

- 2 cups fresh strawberries, hulled and chopped
- 1 cup granulated sugar
- 1/4 cup cocoa powder
- 1 tablespoon lemon juice
- 1 teaspoon vanilla extract
- 2 squares (about 1 ounce) of dark chocolate (70% cocoa or higher), finely chopped
- Zest of one orange (for a citrusy bitter note)

Instructions

1. In a saucepan, combine strawberries, sugar, and lemon juice. Cook over medium heat until strawberries release their juices and the mixture thickens.

2. Stir in cocoa powder and continue cooking until the mixture reaches a jam-like consistency.

3. Add finely chopped dark chocolate, stirring until melted, to introduce a rich bitter chocolate flavor.

4. Stir in vanilla extract and orange zest for an additional layer of bitterness and citrusy flavor.

5. Remove from heat and allow the marmalade to cool before transferring it to sterilized jars. Refrigerate once cooled.

Nutty Blue Cheese Chocolate Spread

Nutty Blue Cheese Chocolate Spread marries the bold creaminess of blue cheese with the richness of dark chocolate, creating a uniquely textured and flavorful spread. This indulgent concoction introduces a delightful crunch with the addition of chopped toasted nuts, such as walnuts or pecans, imparting a savory, nutty complexity to the sweet and tangy base.

Ideal for spreading on artisanal bread, crackers, or as a surprising dip for fresh fruit, the spread transforms ordinary snacks into gourmet experiences. As a topping for warm baguette slices or a filling for stuffed pastries, its savory-sweet profile adds a sophisticated twist to appetizers. Nutty Blue Cheese Chocolate Spread promises a memorable taste adventure, inviting culinary enthusiasts to explore the unconventional yet harmonious blend of flavors in both sweet and savory applications.

Ingredients

- 1/2 cup blue cheese, crumbled
- 1/2 cup dark chocolate, finely chopped (70% cocoa or higher)
- 2 tablespoons cream cheese, softened
- 1 tablespoon honey
- 1/4 cup chopped toasted nuts (such as walnuts or pecans)

Instructions

1. In a bowl, combine blue cheese, dark chocolate, cream cheese, and honey. Mix until well combined and smooth.

2. Fold in the nuts and refrigerate before serving.

Spiced Pomegranate Chocolate Sauce

Spiced Pomegranate Chocolate Sauce elevates the classic with a tantalizing blend of flavors. This velvety sauce seamlessly combines the deep richness of dark chocolate with the vibrant notes of pomegranate, while a hint of ground cinnamon and a pinch of cayenne pepper add a warm, spicy complexity. The result is a sauce that balances sweetness, tartness, and heat in every luscious spoonful. Ideal as a drizzle over desserts like ice cream, cakes, or brownies, it transforms simple treats into gourmet delights.

Use it to elevate breakfast favorites like waffles or pancakes, or as a decadent dip for fresh fruits. The Spiced Pomegranate Chocolate Sauce adds a sophisticated touch to your culinary creations, turning ordinary dishes into extraordinary indulgences.

Ingredients

- 1 cup pomegranate juice
- 1/2 cup dark chocolate chips or chopped dark chocolate (70% cocoa or higher)
- 2 tablespoons honey or maple syrup
- 1 teaspoon vanilla extract
- 1/2 teaspoon ground cinnamon
- Pinch of cayenne pepper (adjust to taste)

Instructions

1. In a saucepan, heat pomegranate juice over medium heat until it simmers.

2. Add dark chocolate, honey or maple syrup, cinnamon, cayenne and vanilla extract. Stir until chocolate is melted and the sauce is smooth.

3.Remove from heat and let it cool before serving.

Smoky Chocolate Dijon Mustard

Indulge your taste buds with the decadent allure of Smoky Chocolate Dijon Mustard. This unconventional blend marries the robust flavor of Dijon mustard with the richness of dark chocolate, creating a uniquely smoky and slightly sweet condiment. The addition of smoked paprika and garlic powder enhances its complexity, offering a versatile culinary experience.

Use it as a tantalizing dip for pretzels or veggies, elevating snack time. Spread it on sandwiches for a gourmet twist or whisk it into salad dressings for a flavor-packed kick. As a grilling glaze, this smoky chocolate concoction transforms ordinary meats into savory delights. Whether drizzled over roasted vegetables or incorporated into marinades, this mustard adds a sophisticated touch to a variety of dishes, showcasing the delightful fusion of smokiness and chocolate sophistication.

Ingredients

- 1/2 cup Dijon mustard
- 2 tablespoons honey
- 2 tablespoons dark chocolate, finely grated or melted
- 1 teaspoon smoked paprika
- 1/2 teaspoon garlic powder
- Salt and pepper to taste

Instructions

1. In a bowl, combine Dijon mustard and honey.

2. Add finely grated or melted dark chocolate to the mustard-honey mixture. Stir well to incorporate.

3. Sprinkle in smoked paprika and garlic powder. Mix thoroughly to evenly distribute the flavors.

4. Season the mustard with salt and pepper according to your taste preferences. Adjust honey or other ingredients if needed.

5. Transfer the Smoky Chocolate Dijon Mustard to a jar or container with a lid.

6. Refrigerate for at least 30 minutes before serving to allow the flavors to meld.

Garlic Infused Caramelized Onion Chocolate Gravy

The Garlic Infused Caramelized Onion Chocolate Gravy is a sensory delight, merging sweet caramelized onions with the savory allure of garlic. The cocoa powder introduces a subtle bittersweet undertone, elevating the gravy into a realm of sophistication. The garlic infusion adds warmth and complexity, creating a nuanced flavor profile that captivates the palate.

This versatile gravy is a culinary revelation, bringing unexpected harmony to classic dishes. Ideal for enhancing mashed potatoes, roast meats, or grilled vegetables, its unique blend of flavors offers a memorable and delightful twist on traditional savory cuisine. The result is a rich and savory chocolate-infused experience that is both comforting and intriguing.

Ingredients

- 2 large onions, thinly sliced
- 3 cloves garlic, minced
- 2 tablespoons butter
- 2 tablespoons all-purpose flour
- 2 cups beef or vegetable broth
- 1/4 cup unsweetened cocoa powder
- 2 tablespoons balsamic vinegar
- Salt and pepper to taste

Instructions

1. In a skillet, melt butter over medium heat. Add thinly sliced onions and minced garlic. Cook until golden brown and fragrant.

2. Sprinkle flour over caramelized onions and garlic, stirring to form a roux. Gradually pour in broth, stirring to avoid lumps. Add cocoa powder and balsamic vinegar, stir until well combined.

3. Let the gravy simmer until desired thickness. Season with salt and pepper to taste.

4. Remove from heat when the gravy thickens. Serve over mashed potatoes, roast meats, or grilled vegetables for a unique twist.

1880s Tomato Chocolate Ketchup

This recipe combines elements reminiscent of the era's flavor profiles but is a product of contemporary culinary imagination rather than a historical document. It is a unique condiment that recalls a time when kitchens embraced unconventional ingredients to elevate traditional recipes. Blending ripe tomatoes, brown sugar, vinegar, and unsweetened chocolate, this ketchup boasted a distinctive taste, marrying sweetness with rich cocoa undertones.

In contemporary kitchens, our 1880s Tomato Chocolate Ketchup , with it's historical charm adds a vintage flair to modern dishes. As a savory-sweet condiment, it enhances burgers, sandwiches, and grilled meats with a sophisticated twist. The fusion of flavors, inspired by the culinary daring of the late 19th century, offers a delightful journey through time, making this Tomato Chocolate Ketchup both a nod to history and a tasteful innovation for today's culinary enthusiasts.

Ingredients

- 2 lbs ripe tomatoes, chopped
- 1 cup brown sugar
- 1 cup apple cider vinegar
- 1 onion, finely chopped
- 1 teaspoon salt
- 1 teaspoon ground cinnamon
- 1/2 teaspoon ground cloves
- 1/4 teaspoon cayenne pepper
- 2 ounces unsweetened chocolate, grated

Elevate your culinary creations by using Tomato Chocolate Ketchup as a glaze for grilled meats, a condiment for burgers, or a unique dipping sauce for appetizers. Its sweet-savory fusion adds a delightful twist to meatloaf, charcuterie boards, and cheese platters. Experiment with this unconventional ketchup in salad dressings and marinades to infuse a rich and complex flavor into your dishes. Its versatility makes it a standout addition to your kitchen, bringing a touch of historical charm with a contemporary twist.

Instructions

1. In a pot, mix 2 lbs chopped tomatoes, 1 cup brown sugar, 1 cup apple cider vinegar, and 1 finely chopped onion.

2. Heat the mixture until tomatoes break down and onion is translucent.

3. Stir in 1 tsp salt, 1 tsp ground cinnamon, 1/2 tsp ground cloves, and 1/4 tsp cayenne pepper.

4. Gradually add 2 oz grated unsweetened chocolate, stirring until melted.

5. Continue simmering until it thickens (about 1-2 hours).

6. Let it cool, then strain through a sieve to remove solids.

7. Transfer to sterilized bottles or jars. Store in a cool place.

Spicy Chocolate BBQ Sauce

The Spicy Chocolate BBQ Sauce offers a tantalizing blend of bold flavors, combining the richness of unsweetened cocoa with a spicy kick. Its deep, smoky undertones from chili powder and smoked paprika complement the sweetness of brown sugar and tanginess of apple cider vinegar. This unique fusion creates a complex, savory-sweet profile with a lingering heat, appealing to adventurous palates.

Ideal for grilling, the sauce transforms ordinary meats into culinary delights. Brush it on chicken, ribs, or burgers during the final grilling moments for an intense burst of flavor. It also serves as a versatile marinade or dipping sauce, elevating dishes with a sophisticated twist. This Spicy Chocolate BBQ Sauce brings a delightful balance of sweet, smoky, and spicy notes, showcasing the creativity that emerges when chocolate meets barbecue in a contemporary culinary experience.

Ingredients

- 1 cup ketchup
- 1/2 cup brown sugar
- 1/4 cup apple cider vinegar
- 1/4 cup water
- 2 tablespoons unsweetened cocoa powder
- 2 tablespoons soy sauce
- 1 tablespoon Dijon mustard
- 1 teaspoon chili powder
- 1/2 teaspoon smoked paprika
- 1/4 teaspoon cayenne pepper (adjust to taste)
- 2 cloves garlic, minced
- Salt and black pepper to taste

Instructions

1. In a saucepan, combine ketchup, brown sugar, apple cider vinegar, water, and cocoa powder. Whisk until smooth.

2. Add soy sauce, Dijon mustard, chili powder, smoked paprika, cayenne pepper, and minced garlic. Stir to combine.

3. Place the saucepan over medium heat and bring the mixture to a simmer.

4. Reduce the heat to low and let the sauce simmer for about 15-20 minutes, stirring occasionally.

5. Season with salt and black pepper to taste. Adjust the spiciness if needed.

6. Remove from heat and let the Spicy Chocolate BBQ Sauce cool before using.

Sweet and Tangy Chocolate Chili Hot Sauce

Experience culinary innovation with our Sweet and Tangy Chocolate Chili Hot Sauce. Infused with cacao nibs, it offers a harmonious blend of heat, subtle sweetness, and nuanced chocolate undertones. Versatile and adventurous, use it to elevate grilled meats, sandwiches, and dips. Brush it on for a flavorful grill finish, or incorporate it into marinades for depth and complexity. Elevate appetizers as a unique dipping sauce or a standout component in cheese platters. This meticulously crafted sauce transforms ordinary dishes into extraordinary delights, bringing an indulgent twist to your contemporary kitchen. Embrace the adventure, explore the possibilities, and savor the exceptional taste that our extraordinary sauce brings to your table.

Ingredients

- 1 cup red chili peppers, chopped
- 4 cloves garlic, minced
- 1 cup apple cider vinegar
- 1/4 cup unsweetened cocoa powder
- 2 tablespoons cacao nibs
- 2 tablespoons olive oil
- 1 teaspoon sugar (adjust to taste)
- 2 tablespoons honey or maple syrup
- 2 tablespoons lime juice
- Salt to taste

Instructions

1. Heat olive oil, sauté garlic.

2. Add chili peppers, cook.

3. Pour vinegar, stir in cocoa, nibs, sugar, honey, lime juice.

4. Simmer 10-15 mins.

5. Blend until smooth.

6. Adjust sweetness, salt.

7. Cool and transfer to a jar.

The choice to retain or strain cacao nibs in the Sweet and Tangy Chocolate Chili Hot Sauce hinges on your preference. Keeping nibs provides texture and boosts chocolate intensity, while straining yields a smoother texture with a slightly subdued chocolate undertone. Select based on your desire for crunchiness and chocolate flavor intensity in the sauce.

Chocolate-Cranberry Chutney

With a bold profile that seamlessly fuses heat, sweetness, and a hint of chocolate sophistication, this hot sauce is a contemporary kitchen essential for those craving memorable and modern flavor experiences.

Indulge your palate with the delectable combination of sweet, tart, and chocolatey notes in Chocolate-Cranberry Chutney. This enticing condiment marries the vibrant flavors of fresh or frozen cranberries with the richness of dark chocolate, creating a harmonious balance. Simmered with orange juice, zest, and a touch of cinnamon, this chutney offers a nuanced and versatile taste experience.

Use it to elevate holiday meals as a delightful accompaniment to roast meats or turkey. Spread it on sandwiches for a gourmet touch or incorporate it into cheese platters to impress guests. The optional addition of chopped nuts introduces a delightful crunch. This Chocolate-Cranberry Chutney is a versatile gem, offering a burst of festive flavors that seamlessly blend the familiar and the unexpected in a culinary symphony.

Ingredients

- 2 cups fresh or frozen cranberries
- 1 cup granulated sugar
- 1/2 cup water
- 1/2 cup orange juice
- Zest of one orange
- 1/2 cup dark chocolate chips or chopped dark chocolate
- 1/4 cup chopped walnuts or pecans (optional)
- 1/2 teaspoon cinnamon
- Pinch of salt

Instructions

1. In a saucepan, combine cranberries, sugar, water, orange juice, and orange zest.

2. Bring the mixture to a boil, then reduce the heat and simmer until the cranberries burst and the sauce thickens (about 10-15 minutes).

3. Stir in dark chocolate chips until melted.

4. Add chopped nuts, if using, cinnamon, and a pinch of salt. Mix well.

Simmer for an additional 5 minutes until the chutney reaches your desired consistency.

Remove from heat and let it cool before transferring to a jar.

Savory Chocolate Pesto

Savory Chocolate Pesto presents a captivating fusion of flavors, where the herbaceous freshness of basil intertwines with the richness of unsweetened cocoa. The toasted pine nuts contribute a subtle nuttiness, complemented by the sharpness of grated Parmesan. The velvety texture, courtesy of extra-virgin olive oil, enhances each bite. A symphony of garlic and citrus notes, derived from lemon zest and juice, adds brightness and depth. The cocoa undertones, though unexpected in a savory context, create a nuanced complexity that lingers on the palate.

This pesto is a delightful marriage of traditional Italian ingredients with a contemporary twist, offering a savory experience with a hint of chocolate sophistication. Versatile and bold, it invites culinary exploration on pasta, sandwiches, or as a distinctive dip.

Ingredients

- 2 cups fresh basil leaves, packed
- 1/2 cup grated Parmesan cheese
- 1/3 cup toasted pine nuts
- 2 cloves garlic, peeled
- 1/2 cup extra-virgin olive oil
- 2 tablespoons unsweetened cocoa powder
- 1/2 teaspoon salt
- 1/4 teaspoon black pepper
- Zest of one lemon
- Juice of half a lemon

Instructions

1. In a food processor, combine basil, Parmesan, pine nuts, and garlic. Pulse until coarsely chopped.

2. With the processor running, slowly pour in the olive oil until the mixture is well blended.

3. Add cocoa powder, salt, black pepper, lemon zest, and lemon juice. Pulse until smooth.

4. Taste and adjust seasoning as needed, adding more salt, pepper, or lemon juice.

5. If the pesto is too thick, you can add more olive oil until you reach your desired consistency.

6. Transfer the Savory Chocolate Pesto to a jar or airtight container.

Chocolate Coffee Steak Sauce

Experience a symphony of flavors in the Date-Infused Chocolate Coffee Steak Sauce—a rich blend of bold coffee, sweet dates, and decadent cocoa. The velvety texture and deep, complex sweetness from the date puree elevate the sauce, creating a luxurious accompaniment for grilled steaks or roasted meats. This unique fusion strikes a perfect balance between savory and sweet, with the coffee adding depth and the cocoa providing a subtle richness.

The sauce's versatility extends beyond steaks; use it as a marinade, dipping sauce, or condiment for a gourmet touch to various dishes. The Date-Infused Chocolate Coffee Steak Sauce offers a culinary journey, where each bite reveals layers of sophisticated and harmonious flavors, transforming everyday meals into extraordinary dining experiences.

Ingredients

- 1 cup strong brewed coffee
- 1/2 cup ketchup
- 1/4 cup soy sauce
- 2 tablespoons Worcestershire sauce
- 2 tablespoons balsamic vinegar
- 1/4 cup dark brown sugar
- 2 tablespoons unsweetened cocoa powder
- 1 teaspoon Dijon mustard
- 2 cloves garlic, minced
- Salt and black pepper to taste
- 1/2 cup pitted and chopped dates
- 1/4 cup red wine (for simmering dates)

Instructions

1. Simmer chopped dates in red wine until soft.

2. Blend the dates and red wine into a smooth puree.

3. In a saucepan, combine coffee, ketchup, soy sauce, Worcestershire sauce, balsamic vinegar, brown sugar, cocoa powder, Dijon mustard, minced garlic, salt, and pepper.

4. Add the date puree to the saucepan mixture.

5. Simmer the combined sauce over low heat for 10-15 minutes.

6. Taste and adjust seasoning as needed.

7. Let the Date-Infused Chocolate Coffee Steak Sauce cool.

8. Serve the cooled sauce over grilled steaks or your preferred meat.

Balsamic Chocolate Fig & Plum Jam

Indulge in the exquisite fusion of flavors with Balsamic Chocolate Fig & Plum Jam. This luscious spread intertwines the sweetness of plums and figs with the depth of balsamic vinegar and the rich undertones of cocoa. The result is a velvety jam that dances on the palate, offering a perfect balance of fruity sweetness and chocolate sophistication. Spread it generously on warm toast for a decadent breakfast, or pair it with creamy cheeses to elevate your charcuterie board. As a versatile condiment, it harmonizes beautifully with grilled meats, adding a sweet and savory dimension.

The Balsamic Chocolate Fig & Plum Jam is not just a condiment; it's a culinary experience, transforming everyday dishes into gourmet delights with its unique and sophisticated flavor profile.

Ingredients

- 2 cups fresh figs, stemmed and chopped
- 1 cup chopped plums
- 1 cup granulated sugar
- 2 tablespoons balsamic vinegar
- 2 tablespoons cocoa powder (unsweetened)
- 1/2 teaspoon vanilla extract

Instructions

1. Combine figs, plums, and sugar in a saucepan. Rest for 30 mins.

2. Heat the mixture over medium heat, stirring to dissolve the sugar. Bring it to a simmer.

3. Reduce heat to medium-low and cook, stirring occasionally, until fruit is soft and mixture thickens (about 30-40 mins).

4. Stir in balsamic vinegar, cocoa powder, and vanilla extract. Simmer for an additional 10-15 mins until desired consistency.

5. Remove the saucepan from heat and let the jam cool for a few minutes.

6. Transfer the jam to sterilized jars, leaving a bit of space at the top.

7. Seal the jars and let them cool completely before refrigerating.

Chunky Chocolate Chipotle Salsa

Dive into a tantalizing experience with Chunky Chocolate Chipotle Salsa, where the smoky heat of chipotle peppers intertwines with the richness of dark chocolate. The texture is a delightful interplay of chunky tomatoes and velvety chocolate chips, complemented by the freshness of cilantro and lime juice.

This salsa captivates the palate with its unique fusion of savory and sweet notes, making it a versatile companion to various dishes. Serve it as a zesty topping for grilled meats, adding a bold kick to your favorite tacos or nachos. Alternatively, savor it with tortilla chips for a mouthwatering snack. The Chunky Chocolate Chipotle Salsa transforms ordinary dishes into extraordinary culinary experiences, revealing layers of complexity that surprise and delight with each savory bite.

Ingredients

- 2 cups diced tomatoes (fresh or canned)
- 1/2 cup red onion, finely chopped
- 1/4 cup fresh cilantro, chopped
- 2 tablespoons canned chipotle peppers in adobo sauce, minced
- 1/4 cup dark chocolate chips
- 2 tablespoons lime juice
- 1 clove garlic, minced
- 1/2 teaspoon ground cumin
- Salt and pepper to taste

Instructions

1. In a mixing bowl, combine diced tomatoes, red onion, cilantro, and minced chipotle peppers.

2. Add dark chocolate chips to the mixture and stir gently to distribute them evenly.

3. Squeeze lime juice over the salsa and add minced garlic, ground cumin, salt, and pepper. Mix well.

4. Allow the salsa to sit for at least 30 minutes to let the flavors meld.

5. Serve the Chunky Chocolate Chipotle Salsa with tortilla chips, grilled meats, or as a flavorful topping for tacos and nachos.

Indonesian Chocolate Tamarind Sauce

Indulge in the exotic allure of Indonesian Chocolate Tamarind Sauce, a culinary symphony that balances sweet, tangy, and rich flavors. The velvety dark chocolate seamlessly melds with the vibrant tamarind, creating a harmonious dance on the palate. The gentle heat from chili flakes adds a subtle kick, while the nuanced sweetness of palm sugar completes this flavorful masterpiece. This sauce elevates grilled meats, tofu, or vegetables, imparting an Indonesian flair to your culinary creations.

Use it as a dipping sauce for skewers or as a glaze for roasted dishes, infusing a depth of complexity that transforms ordinary meals into extraordinary delights. The Indonesian Chocolate Tamarind Sauce is a culinary adventure, inviting you to explore the enchanting world of Indonesian flavors with every savory and indulgent bite.

Ingredients

- 1 cup tamarind paste
- 1/2 cup palm sugar, grated (you can substitute brown sugar)
- 1/4 cup dark chocolate, finely chopped
- 2 tablespoons sweet soy sauce (kecap manis)
- 1 tablespoon soy sauce
- 1 teaspoon tamarind concentrate
- 2 cloves garlic, minced
- 1 teaspoon ginger, grated
- 1 teaspoon chili flakes (adjust to taste)
- 1 tablespoon vegetable oil
- Salt to taste

Instructions

1. In a saucepan, heat vegetable oil over medium heat. Add minced garlic and grated ginger, sauté until fragrant.

2. Add tamarind paste, grated palm sugar, dark chocolate, sweet soy sauce, soy sauce, and tamarind concentrate. Stir well.

3. Allow the mixture to simmer over low heat, stirring frequently, until the chocolate is melted and the sauce thickens.

4. Add chili flakes and salt to taste. Adjust sweetness and spiciness according to your preference.

5. Once the sauce reaches the desired consistency, remove it from heat.

6. Let the Indonesian Chocolate Tamarind Sauce cool before serving.

Honey-Ginger Soy Chocolate Glaze

The Honey-Ginger Soy Chocolate Glaze offers a harmonious blend of contrasting yet complementary flavors. The dark chocolate introduces a rich and velvety sweetness, while the soy sauce provides a subtle umami depth. The addition of honey contributes a delicate floral sweetness that perfectly intertwines with the warmth of freshly minced ginger. This glaze strikes a delicate balance between sweet, savory, and aromatic notes, creating a versatile condiment suitable for both savory and sweet dishes.

Whether drizzled over grilled meats, roasted vegetables, or desserts, the glaze imparts a unique and nuanced flavor profile that elevates every bite. The distinct combination of honey, ginger, soy, and chocolate adds a touch of sophistication to your culinary creations, making it a delightful addition to your repertoire of flavors.

Ingredients

-1/2 cup dark chocolate, finely chopped
- 2 tablespoons soy sauce
- 2 tablespoons honey
- 1 teaspoon finely minced fresh ginger
- 1/4 cup water
- Pinch of salt

Instructions

1. In a small saucepan, combine finely chopped dark chocolate, soy sauce, honey, minced ginger, water, and a pinch of salt.

2. Place the saucepan over low heat and stir continuously until the chocolate is completely melted and the ingredients are well combined.

3. Continue to simmer the glaze over low heat for about 5-7 minutes, stirring occasionally, until it thickens to your desired consistency.

4. Remove the saucepan from heat and let the glaze cool slightly.

5. Taste and adjust the sweetness or add more minced ginger if desired.

6. Once cooled to your liking, drizzle the Honey-Ginger Soy Chocolate Glaze over grilled meats, vegetables, or use it as a delightful topping for desserts.

Matcha Chocolate Teriyaki Sauce

Discover a unique culinary experience with Matcha Chocolate Teriyaki Sauce, a symphony of flavors that marries traditional Japanese elements with a contemporary twist. The subtle bitterness of matcha complements the rich depth of dark chocolate, creating a sauce that unfolds with earthy and velvety notes. Soy and sake contribute umami complexity, while mirin adds a gentle sweetness.

This versatile sauce goes beyond the ordinary, transforming grilled meats into culinary delights or imparting a creative touch to vegetable dishes. Explore its traditional use in sushi or elevate your dipping experience with a sauce that harmonizes nuanced tastes. Matcha Chocolate Teriyaki Sauce is a culinary journey, celebrating the fusion of flavors in a way that respects tradition while embracing a modern palate.

Ingredients

- 1/2 cup soy sauce
- 1/4 cup mirin (sweet rice wine)
- 2 tablespoons sake
- 2 tablespoons matcha powder
- 2 tablespoons dark brown sugar
- 1 tablespoon dark chocolate, finely chopped
- 1 clove garlic, minced
- 1 teaspoon fresh ginger, grated

Instructions

1. In a small saucepan, combine soy sauce, mirin, sake, matcha powder, dark brown sugar, minced garlic, and grated ginger.

2. Place the saucepan over medium heat, stirring to dissolve the sugar. Bring the mixture to a gentle simmer.

3. Once simmering, add finely chopped dark chocolate to the sauce. Stir continuously until the chocolate is completely melted and well incorporated.

4. Continue to simmer for about 5-7 minutes until the sauce thickens to your desired consistency.

5. Remove from heat and let the Matcha Chocolate Teriyaki Sauce cool slightly before using.

Honey Mustard Dark Chocolate Dipping Sauce

Indulge in the decadent allure of this complex Honey Mustard Dark Chocolate Dipping Sauce. The rich and velvety dark chocolate intertwines with the bold Dijon mustard, creating a harmonious balance of sweet and savory notes. Balsamic vinegar adds a subtle tang, while soy sauce and Worcestershire sauce infuse umami depth. The delicate heat from cayenne pepper and smoky undertones of paprika elevate the flavor profile. Finished with a touch of cream, this sauce boasts a luxuriously smooth texture.

Drizzle over grilled meats for a gourmet twist, use as a dipping sauce for pretzels, or elevate cheese platters with its unique sophistication. Versatile and refined, this Honey Mustard Dark Chocolate Dipping Sauce transforms ordinary dishes into extraordinary culinary experiences, unveiling layers of complexity in every delectable bite.

Ingredients

- 1/2 cup dark chocolate, finely chopped
- 1/4 cup Dijon mustard
- 2 tablespoons honey
- 1 tablespoon balsamic vinegar
- 1 tablespoon soy sauce
- 1 teaspoon Worcestershire sauce
- 1 clove garlic, minced
- 1/2 teaspoon smoked paprika
- 1/4 teaspoon cayenne pepper
- Freshly ground black pepper, to taste
- 2 tablespoons heavy cream

Instructions

1. In a small saucepan, melt finely chopped dark chocolate over low heat, stirring continuously until smooth.

2. Add Dijon mustard, honey, balsamic vinegar, soy sauce, Worcestershire sauce, minced garlic, smoked paprika, cayenne pepper, and black pepper to the melted chocolate. Stir well to combine.

3. Gradually add the heavy cream while stirring, ensuring a smooth and velvety texture.

4. Continue to heat the mixture over low heat for an additional 3-5 minutes, allowing the flavors to meld.

5. Taste and adjust the seasoning, sweetness, or spiciness according to your preference.

6. Remove from heat and let cool slightly before serving.

Chocolate Honey Mustard Marinade

Immerse your palate in the luxurious fusion of flavors offered by this Chocolate Honey Mustard Marinade. The velvety dark chocolate harmonizes with the zesty Dijon mustard, creating a symphony of sweet and savory notes. Balsamic vinegar adds a subtle tang, while the complex blend of spices, from smoked paprika to cinnamon, elevates the marinade to gourmet heights. With a hint of heat from cayenne pepper and the richness of olive oil, this marinade is a culinary masterpiece.

Marinate chicken or pork to unlock a depth of flavors, then grill, roast, or bake to perfection. The result is a succulent and sophisticated dish, where each bite reveals layers of complexity and indulgence. Elevate your culinary repertoire with this Chocolate Honey Mustard Marinade, transforming ordinary meats into extraordinary culinary delights.

Ingredients

- 1/2 cup dark chocolate, finely chopped
- 1/4 cup Dijon mustard
- 3 tablespoons honey
- 2 tablespoons balsamic vinegar
- 1 tablespoon soy sauce
- 1 tablespoon Worcestershire sauce
- 2 cloves garlic, minced
- 1 teaspoon smoked paprika
- 1/2 teaspoon cayenne pepper
- 1/2 teaspoon ground coriander
- 1/4 teaspoon ground cinnamon
- Freshly ground black pepper, to taste
- 1/3 cup olive oil

Instructions

1. Melt dark chocolate in a saucepan over low heat, stirring until smooth.

2. In a bowl, combine melted chocolate with Dijon mustard, honey, balsamic vinegar, soy sauce, minced garlic, smoked paprika, cayenne pepper, ground coriander, ground cinnamon, and black pepper. Mix thoroughly.

3. Gradually whisk in olive oil until the marinade is smooth.

4. Allow the marinade to cool slightly before using.

5. Marinate your choice of meats (chicken or pork) for at least 2 hours or overnight in the refrigerator.

6. Grill, roast, or bake the marinated meats for a flavorful and sophisticated dish.

Pear, Onion, Rosemary and Chocolate Marinade

Indulge in the sophistication of the Rosemary Elegance Pear and Chocolate Marinade with Onion, a culinary symphony that harmonizes sweet, savory, and herbal notes. The luscious sweetness of ripe pear intertwines with the rich, velvety essence of dark chocolate. The aromatic touch of rosemary elevates the marinade, adding a layer of herbal elegance. As it graces your choice of meats, be it chicken or pork, the marinade imparts a nuanced flavor profile that unfolds with each bite. Grill, roast, or bake to perfection, unlocking a culinary creation that transcends the ordinary.

The Rosemary addition lends itself to sophisticated dishes, transforming the dining experience into a journey of exquisite taste. Let this marinade redefine your culinary endeavors, offering a fusion of flavors that captivate the senses.

Ingredients

- 1 ripe pear, peeled and finely grated
- 2 tablespoons dark chocolate, finely chopped
- 1/4 cup red wine vinegar
- 1/4 cup olive oil
- 1 tablespoon honey
- 1 small onion, finely chopped
- 2 cloves garlic, minced
- 1 teaspoon fresh rosemary leaves (or 1/2 teaspoon dried rosemary)
- Salt and pepper to taste

Instructions

1. In a bowl, combine grated pear, chopped dark chocolate, red wine vinegar, olive oil, honey, chopped onion, minced garlic, fresh rosemary leaves (or dried rosemary), salt, and pepper. Mix thoroughly.

2. Use the marinade to marinate your choice of meats, such as chicken or pork, for at least 2 hours or overnight in the refrigerator.

3. Grill, roast, or bake the marinated meats for a unique and flavorful dish.

Chocolate Tomato Jam Layer Cake

This exceptional dessert challenges conventional expectations by marrying the robustness of chocolate with the fruity allure of tomato jam, resulting in a captivating symphony of flavors. The foundation of this culinary adventure involves classic ingredients – flour, sugar, cocoa, eggs, milk, and vanilla. What sets it apart is the surprising addition of boiling water, contributing to a thin yet sumptuous batter. Through the alchemy of baking, these elements transform into two indulgent layers that promise a moist and rich experience.

The sweet-tangy twist in this journey comes from the tomato jam – a fusion of tomatoes, sugar, lemon juice, and zest. This delightful concoction undergoes an innovative transformation in a saucepan, thickening into a sweet-tangy jam that adds nuanced complexity. The natural sugars of the tomato elegantly complement the chocolate's richness, creating a dance of flavors that surprises and delights the palate.

Ingredients

For the Chocolate Cake:

- 2 cups all-purpose flour
- 1 and 3/4 cups granulated sugar
- 3/4 cup unsweetened cocoa powder
- 1 and 1/2 teaspoons baking powder
- 1 and 1/2 teaspoons baking soda
- 1 teaspoon salt
- 2 large eggs
- 1 cup whole milk
- 1/2 cup vegetable oil
- 2 teaspoons vanilla extract
- 1 cup boiling water

For the Tomato Jam:

- 2 cups chopped tomatoes
- 1 cup granulated sugar
- 1 tablespoon lemon juice
- 1 teaspoon lemon zest

For the Chocolate Ganache Frosting:

- 1 cup heavy cream
- 8 ounces dark chocolate, finely chopped
- 2 tablespoons unsalted butter

Chocolate Tomato Jam Layer Cake (continued)

The glossy finale crowning this creation is the chocolate ganache frosting, a luxurious blend of heavy cream and dark chocolate with a final buttery note. This velvety texture wraps the cake layers, creating a decadent ensemble beckoning to be savored. The interplay of these elements results in a dessert transcending the ordinary, inviting a celebration of culinary creativity.

The Chocolate Tomato Jam Layer Cake defies culinary norms with its unconventional fusion, offering a symphony of contrasting yet harmonious flavors. This creation extends an invitation to both seasoned bakers and adventurous novices, urging them to embrace creativity. Beyond a dessert, it represents an initiation into a delightful culinary journey, underscoring the pleasures of experimentation. In a world accustomed to predictable tastes, this extraordinary cake sparks conversations, encouraging diners to relish the unexpected. It stands as a testament to the notion that the most extraordinary culinary experiences often emerge unexpectedly.

Instructions

Chocolate Cake:
1. Preheat oven to 350°F (175°C). Grease and flour two 9-inch round cake pans.

2. In a big bowl, mix flour, sugar, cocoa, baking powder, baking soda, and salt.

3. Add eggs, milk, oil, and vanilla. Beat until well combined.

4.Gradually add boiling water, mix until smooth. Batter will be thin.

5. Divide evenly into pans, bake 30-35 mins until a toothpick comes out clean.

6. Let cakes cool completely.

Tomato Jam:
1. In a saucepan, mix tomatoes, sugar, lemon juice, and zest.

2. Cook on medium heat, stirring until jam-like (20-25 mins).

3. Let tomato jam cool.

Chocolate Ganache Frosting:
1. Heat cream until it begins to boil. Pour hot cream over chopped chocolate, let it sit.

2. Stir until smooth, add butter, stir until glossy.

Assemble Cake:
1. Put one cake layer on a plate. Spread tomato jam.

2. Place the second layer, cover with chocolate ganache.

Peppercorn and Chocolate *Panna Cotta*

In the realm of culinary innovation, Peppercorn and Chocolate *Panna Cotta* emerges as a masterpiece, crafting a symphony of flavors that dances on the palate. This daring fusion marries the velvety richness of dark chocolate with the bold, aromatic allure of whole black peppercorns. Each carefully orchestrated spoonful delivers an indulgent yet surprising experience—a harmonious blend where the subtlety of the *panna cotta* meets the assertive heat of the crushed peppercorns.

This unique dessert transcends the ordinary, elevating the classic Italian treat to new heights. It's not merely a dish; it's an exploration, an artistic expression that tantalizes taste buds and leaves an enduring impression—a testament to the boundless creativity and endless possibilities within the world of culinary delights.

Ingredients

- 2 cups heavy cream
1 cup whole milk
1/2 cup granulated sugar
4 ounces dark chocolate, finely chopped
1 teaspoon whole black peppercorns
2 teaspoons gelatin powder
2 tablespoons cold water
1 teaspoon vanilla extract

Instructions

1. In a saucepan, combine heavy cream, whole milk, and sugar. Heat over medium heat, stirring until sugar dissolves.

2. Add dark chocolate to the mixture, stirring until fully melted. Crush peppercorns slightly to release their flavor and add them to the saucepan. Simmer for 5 minutes, then remove from heat.

3. In a small bowl, sprinkle gelatin over cold water. Allow it to bloom for 5 minutes.

4. Strain the peppercorns from the chocolate mixture and return it to low heat. Add the bloomed gelatin, stirring until fully dissolved.

5. Remove from heat and stir in vanilla extract.

6. Pour the mixture into individual molds or glasses. Let it cool to room temperature, then refrigerate for at least 4 hours or until set.

Long Pepper, Chocolate and Mace Parfait

Our Long Pepper, Chocolate, and Mace Parfait is a culinary marvel that unveils a symphony of flavors in each delightful spoonful. This indulgent dessert seamlessly melds the robust warmth of freshly ground long pepper with the velvety richness of dark chocolate and the subtle, aromatic allure of ground mace. The result is a harmonious blend that elevates the classic parfait to new heights of sophistication.

As you savor this exquisite creation, the earthy notes of long pepper dance alongside the deep richness of chocolate, creating a uniquely balanced and indulgent experience. The hint of mace adds a layer of complexity, turning each bite into a journey of sensory delight. Perfect for those seeking a dessert adventure, this parfait is a testament to the artistry of flavor pairing and the endless possibilities within the world of culinary creativity.

Ingredients

- 2 cups heavy cream
- 1 cup whole milk
- 1/2 cup granulated sugar
- 6 ounces dark chocolate, finely chopped
- 1 teaspoon long pepper, freshly ground
- 1/2 teaspoon mace, ground
- 4 large egg yolks
- 1 teaspoon vanilla extract
- Pinch of salt

Instructions

1. Heat cream, milk, and sugar in a saucepan until simmering. Remove from heat.

2. Add chopped dark chocolate, long pepper, and ground mace to the hot mixture. Stir until chocolate melts.

3. In a bowl, whisk egg yolks. Slowly pour some hot mixture into the eggs, whisking continuously. Gradually add the tempered egg mixture back into the saucepan, stirring constantly.

4. Cook the mixture over low heat until it thickens and coats the back of a spoon.

5. Remove from heat, stir in vanilla extract, and add a pinch of salt.

6. Strain the mixture to remove any solids and let it cool to room temperature.

7. Once cooled, pour the mixture into parfait glasses or molds. Refrigerate for at least 4 hours or until set.

Bitter Chocolate No-Bake Cheesecake

Bitter Chocolate No-Bake Cheesecake is an exquisite treat that harmonizes rich flavors and effortless preparation. The luscious chocolate cookie crust, formed from a blend of crumbs and melted butter, provides the perfect base. The creamy filling, a velvety fusion of cream cheese, powdered sugar, and vanilla, is elevated by the addition of melted bitter chocolate, delivering an intense cocoa experience. The airy whipped cream further enhances the texture, creating a sumptuous delight that requires no baking.

Chilled to perfection, this cheesecake sets to a flawless consistency, ensuring a decadent bite with every forkful. For a finishing touch, optional chocolate shavings crown this dessert with elegance. Perfect for those who crave a sophisticated chocolate indulgence, this no-bake masterpiece guarantees a rich and satisfying finale to any occasion.

Ingredients

- 1 1/2 cups chocolate cookie crumbs
- 1/2 cup unsalted butter, melted
- 3 cups cream cheese, softened
- 1 cup powdered sugar
- 1 teaspoon vanilla extract
- 8 ounces bitter chocolate, melted (80% or more)
- 1 1/2 cups heavy cream
- Chocolate shavings for garnish (optional)

Instructions

1. In a bowl, combine chocolate cookie crumbs and melted butter. Press the mixture into the base of a springform pan to form the crust. Chill in the refrigerator while preparing the filling.

2. In a large bowl, beat the softened cream cheese until smooth. Add powdered sugar and vanilla extract, continue beating until well combined.

3. Fold in the melted bitter chocolate until the mixture is uniformly chocolatey.

4. In a separate bowl, whip the heavy cream until stiff peaks form. Gently fold the whipped cream into the chocolate cream cheese mixture until smooth and well incorporated.

4. Pour the filling over the chilled crust in the springform pan, spreading it evenly.

5. Refrigerate for at least 4 hours or until set.

English Oak Barrel Brownie Cake

Our Old and New "English Oak Barrel Brownie Cake" – a culinary revelation promising an unparalleled taste adventure. This dense flavor bomb weaves together the sumptuous depths of dark chocolate, hearty oats, and a carefully curated medley of dried fruits, offering a symphony of textures from the crunch of robust nuts to the chewiness of fruit bits. Elevated by the comforting warmth of bourbon or dark rum, this creation resonates with the sophistication akin to sipping a meticulously aged English oak barrel spirit.

Each indulgent bite is a journey, leaving a lasting imprint on your palate. Discover an exquisite fusion of European inspiration, establishing a fresh tradition of tastes that transcend the ordinary. As you relish every slice, the cake becomes a celebration of flavors, a testament to the intricate dance of ingredients that transforms each moment into an irresistible indulgence, a new standard in dessert sophistication..

Ingredients

- 1 cup unsalted butter
- 1 cup dark chocolate, (60% or more) chopped
- 1 cup brown sugar
- 3 large eggs
- 1 cup all-purpose flour
- 1 cup oats
- 1/2 cup cocoa powder
- 1/4 teaspoon baking powder (reduce for denser texture)
- 1/4 teaspoon salt
- 1/2 cup mixed dried fruits (such as raisins, currants, chopped dates)
- 1/2 cup chopped nuts (such as walnuts or pecans)
- 1/2 cup bourbon or dark rum

Instructions

1. Preheat your oven to 350°F (175°C). Grease and line a square baking pan with parchment paper, leaving a n overhang for easy removal.

2. In a saucepan over low heat, melt butter and dark chocolate until smooth. Let it cool slightly. Add brown sugar and mix well. Beat in eggs one at a time.

3. In a separate bowl, whisk together flour, oats, cocoa powder, a bit of baking powder, and salt.

4. Gradually add the dry mix to the wet, folding in dried fruits and chopped nuts.

5. Stir in bourbon or dark rum until well combined.

6. Pour the batter into the prepared pan and bake for 25-30 minutes or until a toothpick comes out with moist crumbs.

7. Allow the cake to cool in the pan for 10 minutes, then transfer to a wire rack to cool completely.

8. Once cooled, cut into squares or bars and enjoy!

Ancient Grain Crackers with Pistachio and Bitter Chocolate Ganache

Embark on a culinary voyage with our Ancient Grain Crackers, adorned with a luxurious Pistachio and Bitter Chocolate Ganache. This innovative recipe redefines tradition, incorporating a blend of spelt, amaranth, and quinoa flour that not only caters to modern nutritional inclinations but also introduces a distinctive textural experience. These thin, golden-brown crackers stand as a testament to the evolving palate, embracing ancient grains for their robust flavors and wholesome appeal.

The Pistachio and Bitter Chocolate Ganache steals the spotlight with its inventive amalgamation of ingredients. The transformation of shelled pistachios into a creamy paste offers a nuanced nuttiness, complemented by the depth of high cocoa content chocolate. The inclusion of honey or maple syrup adds natural sweetness, while coconut cream introduces a luscious, dairy-free element.

Ingredients

For Ancient Grain Crackers:

- 1 cup ancient grain flour blend (e.g., spelt, amaranth, quinoa)
- 1/4 cup olive oil
- 1/4 cup water
- 1/2 teaspoon salt
- 1 tablespoon sesame seeds (optional for topping)

For Pistachio and Bitter Chocolate Ganache:

- 1/2 cup shelled pistachios
- 100g dark chocolate (70% cocoa or higher), finely chopped
- 1/4 cup honey or maple syrup
- 1/4 cup coconut cream (thick part from a can of coconut milk)
- A pinch of sea salt

Ancient Grain Crackers with Pistachio and Bitter Chocolate Ganache (continued)

This ganache, finished with a pinch of sea salt, achieves a delicate equilibrium of flavors—each component contributing to a sensory symphony that resonates with the discerning tastes of the contemporary consumer.

Beyond its rich flavors, this recipe aligns seamlessly with the modern preference for clean and recognizable ingredients. The choice of coconut cream accommodates diverse dietary preferences, making this treat inclusive and health-conscious. In essence, these Ancient Grain Crackers with Pistachio and Bitter Chocolate Ganache exemplify culinary innovation by blending time-honored ingredients with modern sensibilities, offering a delectable and sophisticated indulgence that captivates the evolving palate of today's culinary enthusiasts.

Instructions

Simple Ancient Grain Crackers:
1. Preheat oven to 350°F (175°C). Mix ancient grain flour, olive oil, water, and salt in a bowl until a dough forms.

2. Roll out the dough thinly on a floured surface.

3. Cut into desired cracker shapes and place on a baking sheet. Optional: Sprinkle sesame seeds on top.

4. Bake for 15-20 minutes or until edges are golden. Cool.

Easy Pistachio Chocolate Ganache:

1. Blend shelled pistachios in a food processor until smooth.

2. Melt dark chocolate using a double boiler or microwave.

3. Combine pistachio paste, melted chocolate, honey/maple syrup, coconut cream, and a pinch of sea salt. Blend until creamy.

Assembly:

1. Spread Pistachio Chocolate Ganache on cooled crackers. Optional: Garnish with chopped pistachios or a sprinkle of sea salt.

2. Allow ganache to set slightly before serving.

Cocoa Nib and Raspberry Fool with Bitter Chocolate *Espuma*

This culinary innovation, the Cocoa Nib and Raspberry Fool with Bitter Chocolate *Espuma*, creates a harmonious symphony of textures and flavors. It effortlessly combines fruity sweetness, cocoa crunch, and velvety foam, epitomizing modern dessert indulgence for a delightful spoonful.

This delectable creation epitomizes both simplicity and sophistication in dessert innovation. The fool, melding fresh raspberries, powdered sugar, cocoa nibs, and whipped cream, effortlessly harmonizes natural sweetness with a bold cocoa crunch. Its airy texture and vibrant flavors beautifully showcase the seamless marriage of these exquisite ingredients, creating an indulgence that transcends the ordinary.

Complementing this fruity indulgence is the Bitter Chocolate *Espuma*, a revelation in culinary techniques. *Espuma*, Spanish for "foam," denotes

Ingredients

For Cocoa Nib and Raspberry Fool:

- 1 cup fresh raspberries
- 2 tablespoons cocoa nibs
- 1/4 cup powdered sugar
- 1 cup heavy cream
- 1 teaspoon vanilla extract

For Bitter Chocolate Espuma:

- 100g dark chocolate (70% cocoa or higher), finely chopped
- 1 cup whole milk
- 2 tablespoons sugar
- 1 teaspoon instant coffee (optional)

Cocoa Nib and Raspberry Fool with Bitter Chocolate *Espuma* (continued)

a light, frothy texture achieved through aeration. The Bitter Chocolate *Espuma* takes classic chocolate indulgence to new heights with melted dark chocolate, whole milk, and sugar forming a velvety base. Optional instant coffee adds depth, creating a frothy delight ready to crown the Raspberry Fool.

This invention blends contrasting elements – the tartness of raspberries, the crunch of cocoa nibs, and the bittersweet sophistication of dark chocolate *espuma*. Assembled with ease, it promises an exquisite experience with minimal effort. Perfect for those seeking a dessert that marries innovation with familiar flavors, this delightful union elevates the art of dessert creation in mere minutes.

Instructions

Super Simple Cocoa Nib and Raspberry Fool:

1. In a bowl, mash fresh raspberries with powdered sugar for a chunky puree.
2. Gently fold in cocoa nibs.
3. Whip heavy cream until soft peaks form.
4. Fold whipped cream into the raspberry mixture.
5. Add vanilla extract and gently combine.
6. Refrigerate for at least 1 hour before serving.

Super Simple Bitter Chocolate Espuma:

1. Melt dark chocolate using a double boiler or microwave.
2. In a saucepan, heat whole milk and sugar until simmering; remove from heat.
3. Add melted chocolate to the milk mixture; whisk until smooth. Optional: Add instant coffee for depth.
4. Allow the mixture to cool, then refrigerate for at least 2 hours.

Assembly:

1. Spoon Cocoa Nib and Raspberry Fool into serving glasses or bowls.
2. Using an immersion blender, whip Bitter Chocolate Espuma until frothy.
3. Top each serving with a generous dollop of chocolate espuma.
Optional: Garnish with more cocoa nibs or fresh raspberries.

Bittersweet Citrus Fusion Mini-Galettes

Embark on a delightful culinary journey with our Bittersweet Citrus Fusion Mini-Galettes, a recipe that harmonizes rich dark chocolate with the sweetness of pears, plums, and a surprising twist of grapefruit. The adventure begins by crafting the perfect galette dough in a food processor, where flour, sugar, and salt converge into a crumbly mixture. Cold butter is introduced, creating a texture that, with the gradual addition of ice water, transforms into a cohesive disk. After a relaxing chill, the dough emerges, promising a tender and flaky crust.

The heart of this gastronomic odyssey lies in the filling—a symphony of sliced pears, plums, and dark chocolate chips. Sugar, cornstarch, vanilla extract, and unexpected grapefruit slices elevate the medley, creating a balance of sweet and bitter notes. The addition of finely grated dark chocolate introduces a sophisticated layer of complexity.

Ingredients

For the Galette Dough:

- 1 1/4 cups all-purpose flour
- 1 tablespoon granulated sugar
- 1/2 teaspoon salt
- 1/2 cup unsalted butter, cold and cut into cubes
- 3-4 tablespoons ice water

For the Filling:

- 1 ripe pear, thinly sliced
- 1 ripe plum, sliced
- 1/4 cup dark chocolate chips or chunks
- 2 tablespoons granulated sugar
- 1 tablespoon cornstarch
- 1 teaspoon vanilla extract
- 1/2 grapefruit, thinly sliced (without peel, and remove seeds)
- A touch of finely grated dark chocolate for bitterness

For Assembly:

- 1 egg (for egg wash)
- Demerara sugar (for sprinkling)

Instructions

Bittersweet Citrus Fusion Mini-Galettes (continued)

Assembling these mini-galettes becomes an art form on a floured surface, where the chilled dough is rolled out into mini circles, embracing the bittersweet citrus-chocolate concoction. The rustic folding of edges creates individual galettes, adorned with an egg wash and a sprinkle of Demerara sugar. In the oven's warm embrace, they bake to a golden brown perfection.

Serving warm or at room temperature, these Bittersweet Citrus Fusion Mini-Galettes invite you to savor the symphony of flavors and textures. Each bite unfolds a delightful blend, showcasing the meticulous dance of sweet and bitter elements. The cooling period allows the flavors to meld, delivering a moment of culinary bliss in this remarkable flavour journey.

1. Prepare the Galette Dough:
- Pulse together flour, sugar, and salt in a food processor.
- Add cold butter and pulse until it resembles coarse crumbs.
- Gradually add ice water until the dough comes together.
- Shape into a disk, wrap in plastic, and chill for 30 minutes.
- Preheat oven to 375°F (190°C).

2. Prepare the Filling:
- Toss pear, plum, chocolate chips, sugar, cornstarch, vanilla, grapefruit slices, and grated dark chocolate in a bowl.

3. Assemble the Galettes:
- Roll out chilled dough into mini circles on a floured surface.
- Place bittersweet citrus-chocolate mixture in the center.
- Fold edges over, creating rustic galette shapes.
- Transfer to parchment-lined baking sheet.

4. Bake:
- Beat egg in a small bowl for an egg wash. Brush edges and sprinkle with Demerara sugar.
- Bake for 20-25 minutes or until golden brown.

5. Serve:
- Allow mini-galettes to cool slightly before serving. Enjoy warm or at room temperature, savoring the sophisticated blend of sweet and bitter notes!

No-Churn Chocolate Spinach Ice Cream

Indulge in the surprising delight of Chocolate Spinach Ice Cream, a harmonious fusion that promises a rich, chocolatey experience with a touch of nutritional goodness. This unique frozen treat combines the decadence of chocolate with the subtle vibrancy of fresh spinach. The result? A creamy, luscious ice cream that tantalizes your taste buds. The chocolate flavor takes center stage, offering a velvety sweetness, while the finely pureed spinach adds a hidden layer of nutrition without compromising the indulgent experience. Blended to perfection, the spinach contributes to the ice cream's smooth texture, creating a guilt-free dessert that not only satisfies your sweet cravings but also provides a sneak peek into the world of innovative and wholesome flavors. Whether you're a chocolate enthusiast or an adventurous dessert connoisseur, Chocolate Spinach Ice Cream is a delightful surprise that brings a nutritious twist to the classic frozen treat.

Ingredients

- 2 cups fresh spinach, washed and stems removed
- 1 cup whole milk
- 2 cups heavy cream
- 1 cup sweetened condensed milk
- 1 cup cocoa powder
- 1 cup chocolate chips or chunks
- 1 teaspoon vanilla extract
- Pinch of salt

Instructions

1. Combine fresh spinach and whole milk in a blender. Blend until the spinach is finely pureed.

2. In a large mixing bowl, combine the spinach-milk mixture, heavy cream, sweetened condensed milk, cocoa powder, chocolate chips, vanilla extract, and a pinch of salt.

3. Use a hand mixer or a whisk to blend all the ingredients thoroughly until you have a smooth and well-combined mixture.

4. Pour the mixture into a lidded container suitable for freezing.

5. Place the container in the freezer and freeze for about 1 hour.

6. After an hour, take it out and whisk vigorously to break up any ice crystals.

7. Repeat this process every hour for the first 3-4 hours.

8. Allow the ice cream to freeze for at least 6 hours or overnight until it reaches a firm consistency.

9. When ready to serve, let the ice cream soften for a few minutes at room temperature, then scoop and enjoy!

Bitter Melon Cocoa Savory Crisps

In this unconventional culinary adventure, bitter melon takes an unexpected turn with a cocoa twist, creating a unique and surprisingly delightful dessert. Thinly sliced bitter melon meets the savory embrace of olive oil before being coated in a rich cocoa blend, transforming its intense bitterness into a complex flavor profile. Baked until crisp, the cocoa-infused slices are then drizzled with honey or maple syrup for a touch of sweetness.

Optional chopped nuts provide a satisfying crunch, completing this oddly enticing fusion of bitter, savory, and sweet notes. A testament to culinary creativity, this dessert challenges expectations and invites the palate to explore the uncharted territory of flavors in a concise and intriguing culinary experiment.

Ingredients

- 1 medium-sized bitter melon, deseeded and thinly sliced
- 2 tablespoons cocoa powder
- 1/4 cup honey or maple syrup
- 1 tablespoon olive oil
- A pinch of sea salt
- Chopped nuts (almonds or walnuts) for garnish (optional)

Instructions

1. Preheat the oven to 375°F (190°C).

2. Place the thinly sliced bitter melon in a bowl.

3. Drizzle olive oil over the slices and toss to coat evenly.

4. In a separate bowl, mix the cocoa powder and a pinch of sea salt.

5. Coat each bitter melon slice with the cocoa mixture, ensuring they are well-covered.

6. Lay the cocoa-coated bitter melon slices on a baking sheet lined with parchment paper.

7. Bake in the preheated oven for 15-20 minutes or until the bitter melon slices are crisp, but not burnt.

8. Once out of the oven, drizzle honey or maple syrup over the cocoa-coated bitter melon slices.

9. If desired, sprinkle chopped nuts (almonds or walnuts) over the top for added texture and flavor.

10. Allow the dessert to cool slightly before serving.

Sesame Seed, Honey & Parmesan Cocoa Crackers

Discover a gourmet journey with our Sesame Seed, Honey & Parmesan Cocoa Crackers. A culinary marvel, these crackers unite the robust bitterness of unsweetened cocoa with the savory allure of grated Parmesan, elevated by the nutty crunch of sesame seeds. The addition of honey introduces a nuanced sweetness, crafting a symphony of flavors that defies expectations. Each bite achieves a perfect balance—crispy edges and a tender interior, sweet notes harmonizing with savory depths.

Beyond mere snacking, these crackers represent a culinary art form, challenging conventions with inventive flavor pairing. Embrace the paradoxical delight of our crackers, where bitterness meets sweetness and crunch marries tenderness. Elevate your palate with this gourmet experience, a testament to the boundless creativity within every nibble.

Ingredients

- 1 cup all-purpose flour
- 1/2 cup unsweetened cocoa powder
- 1/2 cup grated Parmesan cheese
- 1/4 cup sesame seeds
- 1 tablespoon honey
- 1/2 teaspoon salt
- 1/2 cup unsalted butter, cold and cut into small cubes
- 3-4 tablespoons cold water

Instructions

1. Preheat your oven to 350°F (175°C) and line a baking sheet with parchment paper.

2. In a large bowl, whisk together flour, cocoa powder, grated Parmesan, sesame seeds, and salt.

3. Add cold, cubed butter to the dry ingredients. Use a pastry cutter or your fingers to incorporate until it resembles coarse crumbs.

4. Drizzle honey over the mixture and mix until the dough starts to come together.

5. Gradually add cold water, one tablespoon at a time, and mix until the dough forms a ball. Be careful not to overmix.

6. On a lightly floured surface, roll out the dough to about 1/8-inch thickness.

7. Use cookie cutters or a knife to cut the dough into desired shapes, and place the cut crackers on the prepared baking sheet.

8. Bake in the preheated oven for 12-15 minutes or until the edges are firm.

9. Allow the crackers to cool on the baking sheet for a few minutes, then transfer them to a wire rack to cool.

Cocoa Chai Popsicles

Embark on a flavor journey with our Cocoa Chai Popsicle—a frozen delight fusing robust cocoa bitterness with the inviting warmth of chai spices. The process unfolds with a fragrant infusion of cinnamon, cardamom, cloves, ginger, and black pepper, creating a chai base. This aromatic elixir gracefully combines with a velvety blend of unsweetened cocoa powder and sweetened condensed milk, achieving a sublime equilibrium of bitter and sweet.

As the popsicles freeze, flavors harmonize into a captivating symphony, delivering a frozen sensation that tantalizes the taste buds. Each lick reveals layers of indulgence, offering a distinctive take on traditional popsicles—an amalgamation of chai's comforting embrace and cocoa's bold allure. Elevate your frozen treat experience with this fusion of spice and chocolate, a refreshingly delightful journey for every palate.

Ingredients

- 1 cup unsweetened cocoa powder
- 1 can (14 ounces) sweetened condensed milk
- 1 1/2 teaspoons ground cinnamon
- 1 teaspoon ground cardamom
- 1/2 teaspoon ground cloves
- 1/2 teaspoon ground ginger
- 1/4 teaspoon ground black pepper
- 2 cups water

Instructions

1. In a small saucepan, mix 2 cups water with ground cinnamon, cardamom, cloves, ginger, and black pepper.

2. Simmer the mixture over medium heat, stirring occasionally.

3. Reduce heat to low and let the spices steep for about 10 minutes.

4. Strain the chai spice infusion, removing the spices, and let it cool to room temperature.

4. In a bowl, whisk together cocoa powder and sweetened condensed milk until well combined.

5. Gradually add the chai spice infusion to the cocoa mixture, stirring continuously for a smooth consistency.

6. Pour the chai-spiced cocoa and condensed milk into popsicle molds, leaving a small space at the top.

7. Freeze the popsicle molds for 4-6 hours or until solid. Once fully frozen, remove the popsicles from the molds and enjoy!

Bitter Chocolate Lavash

Experience the pinnacle of culinary refinement with our Bitter Chocolate Lavash Flatbread. This innovative recipe seamlessly blends the time-honored charm of traditional lavash with the bold allure of bitter cocoa and dark chocolate, crafting a decadent flatbread that achieves a perfect balance. The rich flavors of unsweetened cocoa powder and finely chopped dark chocolate meld together, creating an exquisite fusion of sweetness and bitterness. Elevate your dining experience with this symphony of tastes, a testament to the harmonious marriage of culinary tradition and modern creativity. Beyond a mere dish, it's an exploration of nuanced complexities, inviting you to indulge in a moment of refined pleasure. Whether enjoyed on its own or paired with accompaniments, our Bitter Chocolate Lavash Flatbread promises a journey for your palate—a celebration of heritage and innovation, a refined indulgence in every bite.

Ingredients

- 2 cups all-purpose flour
- 1/2 cup unsweetened cocoa powder
- 1 teaspoon baking powder
- 1/2 teaspoon salt
- 1 tablespoon granulated sugar
- 1 cup warm water
- 2 tablespoons olive oil
- 1 teaspoon vanilla extract
- 1/2 cup dark chocolate, finely chopped

Instructions

1. Preheat your oven to 375°F (190°C). Line a baking sheet with parchment paper.

2. In a large mixing bowl, whisk together the all-purpose flour, cocoa powder, baking powder, salt, and granulated sugar.

3. Create a well in the center of the dry ingredients and pour in the warm water, olive oil, and vanilla extract. Mix until a dough forms.

4. Turn the dough out onto a floured surface and knead for about 5 minutes or until it becomes smooth and elastic.

5. Incorporate the finely chopped dark chocolate into the dough, ensuring it is evenly distributed.

6. Cover the dough with a damp cloth and let it rest for 15-20 minutes to allow the gluten to relax.

7. Divide the dough into smaller portions. Roll each portion into a thin sheet, aiming for a flatbread-like consistency.

Bitter Cocoa & Prune Compote for Lavash

Meticulously crafted from premium unsweetened cocoa powder, organic granulated sugar, and finely chopped dark chocolate, our Bitter Cocoa and Prune Compote orchestrates a fusion of intense bitterness and luxurious sweetness. Enriched with warm maple syrup, vanilla extract, and a hint of ground cinnamon, it offers a symphony of sophisticated flavors. For an extra thrill, a dash of cayenne pepper provides a subtle kick, complemented by chewy chopped prunes.

As it simmers, this compote magically transforms into a luscious treat, transcending the ordinary. Versatile and decadent, it's the perfect enhancement for desserts, pancakes, or ice cream, inviting you to elevate your culinary creations with its bold and refined taste.

8. Place the rolled-out flatbreads on the prepared baking sheet and bake for 12-15 minutes or until the edges are crisp.

9. Allow the Bitter Chocolate Lavash Flatbread to cool on a wire rack before serving.

For the Compote

Ingredients

- 1/2 cup high-quality unsweetened cocoa powder
- 1/2 cup organic granulated sugar
- 1 cup water
- 1/4 cup quality dark chocolate, finely chopped
- 2 tablespoons pure maple syrup
- 1 teaspoon pure vanilla extract
- 1/2 teaspoon ground cinnamon
- A pinch of cayenne pepper (optional)
- A pinch of sea salt
- 1/2 cup pitted prunes, chopped

Instructions

1. In a saucepan, mix cocoa powder, sugar, water, dark chocolate, maple syrup, vanilla extract, cinnamon, cayenne pepper (optional), and a pinch of sea salt.

2. Heat the mixture on low, stirring until chocolate melts and ingredients combine.

3. Add chopped prunes, stir to incorporate.

4. Simmer gently until prunes soften, and the mixture thickens.

5. Cool the compote; it thickens as it cools.

Pies, Cakes & Pastries

Cocoa-Dusted Brandy Infused Spoonbread with Stewed Gooseberries and Dark Chocolate Shavings

Indulge in a sublime culinary experience with our Cocoa-Dusted Brandy-Infused Spoonbread Verrine featuring stewed gooseberries and dark chocolate shavings. A verrine is a stylish serving technique where layers of complementary flavors are artfully assembled in a glass or small dish, providing a visual and gastronomic delight.

This dessert begins with a decadent gooey brandy spoonbread, a harmonious blend of cornmeal, flour, and brandy, achieving a rich and moist texture. The spoonbread is skillfully cut into bite-sized cubes, forming the foundation of the verrine. Stewed gooseberries, sweet and tart, contribute a luscious layer that complements the intense gooey texture of the spoonbread. Their natural sweetness is enhanced with a touch of sugar, creating a balanced and vibrant fruit component.

Ingredients

Gooey Brandy Spoonbread
- 1 cup cornmeal
- 1 cup all-purpose flour
- 1/2 cup sugar
- 1 tablespoon baking powder
- 1/2 teaspoon salt
- 1 cup milk
- 1/2 cup unsalted butter, melted
- 3 large eggs
- 1/4 cup brandy
- 1 teaspoon vanilla extract

Stewed Gooseberries:
- Fresh or frozen gooseberries (enough for a generous layer in the verrine)
- Sugar (to taste, for stewing the gooseberries)

Verrine Assembly:
- Cocoa powder (for dusting)
- Dark chocolate (70% cocoa or higher, for shaving)

Instructions

For Gooey Brandy Spoonbread:

1. Preheat your oven to 375°F (190°C) and grease a baking dish.

2. In a mixing bowl, combine cornmeal, flour, sugar, baking powder, and salt.

3. In another bowl, whisk together milk, melted butter, eggs, brandy, and vanilla extract. Add wet ingredients to dry ingredients, mixing until just combined.

4. Pour the batter into the greased baking dish and bake for about 25-30 minutes or until set and golden brown. Allow it to cool.

Cocoa-Dusted Brandy Infused Spoonbread with Stewed Gooseberries and Dark Chocolate Shavings (continued)

To elevate the experience, the verrine is adorned with a dusting of cocoa powder, imparting a subtle bitterness that perfectly counterbalances the sweetness. The addition of dark chocolate shavings introduces a sophisticated and bitter note, preventing the dessert from becoming overly saccharine.

The small, thoughtfully portioned verrine ensures that each spoonful delivers a harmonious blend of flavors without overwhelming the palate. The careful interplay of gooey texture, sweet gooseberries, and bitter cocoa and chocolate creates a dessert that is not only visually appealing but also a symphony of tastes in every delectable bite. Immerse yourself in this culinary masterpiece, where each layer harmonizes to create a dessert that is as delightful to the eyes as it is to the taste buds.

For Stewed Gooseberries:

1. In a saucepan, combine gooseberries with sugar to taste.

2. Cook over medium heat, stirring occasionally, until gooseberries soften and release their juices. This can take about 10-15 minutes.
3. Adjust sweetness according to your preference.

Verrine Assembly:

1. Cut the gooey brandy spoonbread into small, bite-sized cubes.

2. In verrine glasses or small serving dishes, layer spoonbread cubes.

3. Spoon a layer of stewed gooseberries on top of the spoonbread layer.

4. Repeat the layers until the verrine is filled, finishing with a layer of gooseberries.

5. Dust the top with cocoa powder.
Dark Chocolate Shavings:

6. Just before serving, use a vegetable peeler to create thin shavings of dark chocolate. Sprinkle the chocolate shavings on top of the verrine to add a delightful bitter note.
Serve:

7. Serve the verrines chilled or at room temperature, allowing the flavors to meld.consistency.

Spiced Red Wine Chocolate Harvest Bread

The chocolate bread, a symphony of flavors featuring apricots, dates, figs, raisins, and sultanas soaked in red wine, infused with cinnamon, star anise, cloves, and ginger, promises a decadent and memorable culinary experience. The first notes to hit the senses are the deep, rich chocolate aroma emanating from the cocoa powder, inviting anticipation with each slice. The mixed dried fruits, steeped in red wine, contribute a natural sweetness and a delightful medley of fruity flavors, offering chewy and tender bites that showcase the unique taste of apricots, dates, figs, raisins, and sultanas.

Complementing this symphony is the red wine infusion, subtly weaving complexity into the overall flavor profile. It introduces a nuanced hint of tartness and an added layer of richness, elevating the bread beyond the ordinary.

Ingredients

- 1 cup mixed dried fruits (apricots, dates, figs, raisins, and sultanas)
- 1 cup red wine
- 1 teaspoon ground cinnamon
- 1 teaspoon ground star anise
- 1/2 teaspoon ground cloves
- 1 teaspoon ground ginger
- 2 cups all-purpose flour
- 1/2 cup cocoa powder
- 1 1/2 teaspoons baking powder
- 1/2 teaspoon baking soda
- 1/2 teaspoon salt
- 1 cup granulated sugar
- 1/2 cup unsalted butter, softened
- 3 large eggs
- 1 teaspoon vanilla extract
- 1/2 cup buttermilk
- 1 cup chocolate chips (optional)

Instructions

1. Preheat your oven to 350°F (175°C). Grease and flour a 9x5-inch loaf pan.

2. In a small saucepan, combine the mixed dried fruits, red wine, ground cinnamon, ground star anise, ground cloves, and ground ginger. Heat over medium heat until the mixture simmers. Let it simmer for about 5 minutes, then remove it from the heat and let it cool. This will allow the dried fruits to soak up the flavors.

3. In a medium bowl, whisk together the all-purpose flour, cocoa powder, baking powder, baking soda, and salt. Set aside.

Spiced Red Wine Chocolate Harvest Bread (continued)

The warm spice blend of cinnamon, star anise, cloves, and ginger intertwines seamlessly, creating a comforting and well-rounded taste that lingers on the palate. This infusion of spices transforms the chocolate bread into a harmonious blend of sweetness, warmth, and chocolatey goodness.

The moist, tender crumb results from buttermilk and soaked dried fruits. Optional chocolate chips, if added, bring melty, gooey pockets enhancing decadence. Balanced sweetness, with granulated sugar, dried fruits, and chocolate chips, allows natural sweetness to shine. Whether enjoyed alone or with butter, this versatile chocolate bread pairs well with coffee or tea, offering a symphony of flavors in each bite.

4. In a large mixing bowl, cream together the softened butter and sugar until light and fluffy. Add the eggs one at a time, beating well after each addition. Stir in the vanilla extract.

5. Gradually add the dry ingredients to the wet ingredients, alternating with the buttermilk. Begin and end with the dry ingredients. Mix until just combined.

6. Fold in the soaked dried fruit mixture and chocolate chips (if using).

7. Pour the batter into the prepared loaf pan and smooth the top with a spatula.

8. Bake in the preheated oven for 60-70 minutes, or until a toothpick inserted into the center comes out clean.

9. Allow the chocolate bread to cool in the pan for 10 minutes, then transfer it to a wire rack to cool completely.

10. Once cooled, slice and enjoy your chocolate bread with a delightful mix of flavors from the infused dried fruits and spices.

Cocoa-Rye Biscuits with Apple Dust

Rooted in centuries-old Nordic culinary traditions, the traditional Kavring recipe has sustained communities through harsh winters. Originating as a robust, tangy rye bread, variations of Kavring have adapted to regional tastes, incorporating an array of spices and sweeteners. Our Cocoa-Rye Biscuits with Apple Dust pay homage to this rich history, infusing a contemporary twist into the Nordic legacy.

Crafted with reverence for the traditional, our biscuits introduce a modern flair with the addition of cocoa. The marriage of cocoa's luscious depth and the rustic notes of rye creates an enticing fusion. Aromatic hints of cinnamon, cloves, and cardamom echo the warm spices found in traditional Kavring, offering a comforting and evocative experience reminiscent of Nordic kitchens.

Ingredients

- 2 cups rye flour
- 1 cup all-purpose flour
- 1/4 cup cocoa powder
- 1 teaspoon baking soda
- 1/2 teaspoon salt
- 1/2 cup unsalted butter, softened
- 1/2 cup brown sugar
- 1/4 cup molasses
- 1 teaspoon ground cinnamon
- 1/2 teaspoon ground cloves
- 1/2 teaspoon ground cardamom
- 1/2 cup buttermilk
- 1/4 cup apple dust (pealed and seeded apples dehydrated and ground in dust or processed with maltodextrin)

Instructions

1. Preheat your oven to 350°F (175°C). Line a baking sheet with parchment paper.

2. In a bowl, whisk together rye flour, all-purpose flour, cocoa powder, baking soda, salt, cinnamon, cloves, and cardamom. Set aside.

3. In a separate large bowl, cream together the softened butter, brown sugar, and molasses until light and fluffy.

4. Gradually add the dry ingredients to the wet ingredients, mixing well. Alternate with buttermilk, starting and ending with the dry ingredients. Mix until just combined.

5. On a floured surface, roll out the dough to about 1/2-inch thickness. Use a biscuit cutter to cut out individual biscuits.

Cocoa-Rye Biscuits with Apple Dust (continued)

Upon indulging, the cocoa aroma immediately captivates, paving the way for a nuanced flavor journey. The initial bite reveals the robust essence of rye, harmonizing with the deep, rich undertones of cocoa. Subtle sweetness from brown sugar and molasses blends seamlessly with the spiced apple dust, creating a delightful interplay of sweet and savory.

The texture is a testament to craftsmanship—each biscuit boasts a firm exterior, encapsulating a moist and tender crumb within. The combination of buttermilk and the carefully selected blend of spices ensures a well-rounded and satisfying taste that lingers on the palate.

These biscuits are a celebration of Nordic resilience and culinary ingenuity, bridging the gap between the past and the present. With every bite, you embark on a culinary voyage, honoring the roots of Kavring while embracing the spirit of contemporary

6. Place the biscuits on the prepared baking sheet and bake for 12-15 minutes, or until the biscuits are firm. Remove from the oven and let them cool slightly.

7. While the biscuits are still warm, brush the surface with melted butter or a simple glaze made with honey or maple syrup.

8. Sprinkle the apple dust over the warm biscuits while the butter or glaze is still wet. Press gently to help the dust adhere.

9. Allow the biscuits to cool completely, allowing the surface treatment (butter or glaze) to solidify and secure the apple dust.

10. If desired, lightly brush a clear edible glaze or syrup over the apple dust to create a seal. This step is optional but can enhance the longevity of the apple dust on the biscuits.

Here are four serving or pairing ideas for the Cocoa-Rye Biscuits with Apple Dust:

1. Apple Butter:
Spread biscuits generously with apple butter for a sweet and spiced delight.

2. Cheddar Cheese:
Pair biscuits with high-quality cheddar cheeses for a savory-sweet contrast.

3. Apple Cider:
Enjoy with warm spiced apple cider for a cozy and seasonal treat.
Ice Cream Indulgence:

4. Vanilla Ice Cream Sandwiches:
 - Turn the biscuits into dessert by sandwiching a scoop of vanilla ice cream between two biscuits. The cold, creamy ice cream contrasts beautifully with the warm, spiced flavors of the biscuits, creating a delightful dessert experience.

Chocolate Avocado Mousse with Sea Salt

Indulge in the luxurious fusion of Chocolate Avocado Mousse with Sea Salt—a contemporary delight merging decadence with health-conscious choices. This innovative dessert marries the creamy richness of avocados with the deep allure of cocoa, creating a velvety mousse that surprises the palate. The addition of a hint of sea salt enhances the complexity, providing a perfect balance of sweet and savory notes. Serve this at parties to captivate guests with a guilt-free, sophisticated treat.

The dish nods to the modern trend of incorporating nutrient-rich ingredients into indulgent desserts, appealing to those seeking both flavor and mindful consumption. The intriguing blend of familiar and unexpected flavors makes it a conversation starter and a memorable addition to any gathering, where culinary sophistication meets wholesome satisfaction.

Ingredients

- 12 ripe avocados, peeled and pitted
- 1/4 cup unsweetened cocoa powder
- 1/4 cup maple syrup or honey (adjust to taste)
- 1/4 cup almond milk or any milk of your choice
- 1 teaspoon vanilla extract
- Pinch of sea salt
- Optional toppings: whipped cream, berries, or additional sea salt for garnish

Instructions

1. Scoop out the flesh of the ripe avocados and place them in a food processor or blender.

2. Add cocoa powder, maple syrup (or honey), almond milk, vanilla extract, and a pinch of sea salt to the avocados.

3. Blend the ingredients until you achieve a smooth and creamy mousse consistency. Scrape down the sides of the blender or food processor as needed.

4. Taste the mousse and adjust sweetness by adding more maple syrup or honey if needed. Blend again to incorporate any adjustments.

5. Transfer the chocolate avocado mousse to serving glasses or bowls. Cover and refrigerate for at least 1-2 hours to chill and allow the flavors to meld.

6. Once chilled, remove from the refrigerator. Top with whipped cream, berries, or a sprinkle of sea salt for a finishing touch.

Black Pepper Chocolate Tart

Embark on a culinary journey with the Black Pepper Chocolate Tart—a unique fusion that marries the ancient spice route with modern indulgence. Historically, spices like black pepper were prized commodities, and their inclusion in desserts echoes a tradition of exotic flavor exploration. This unconventional pairing, where the piquancy of freshly ground black pepper harmonizes with the richness of dark chocolate, results in a sophisticated and intriguing taste experience. The pepper's subtle heat complements the sweetness, creating a symphony of flavors on the palate.

The Black Pepper Chocolate Tart stands as a testament to the adventurous spirit of gastronomy, urging taste buds to savor the unexpected. Delight in this odd yet delightful combination, where the past meets the present, and flavors intertwine in a celebration of culinary curiosity.

Ingredients

For the Crust:
- 1 1/2 cups chocolate cookie crumbs
- 1/3 cup melted butter
- 2 tablespoons sugar

For the Filling:
- 1 1/2 cups heavy cream
- 8 ounces dark chocolate, finely chopped
- 2 tablespoons unsalted butter
- 1 teaspoon vanilla extract
- 1/2 teaspoon freshly ground black pepper
- Pinch of salt

For Garnish (Optional):
- Whipped cream
- Freshly ground black pepper

Instructions

For the Crust:
1. Preheat the oven to 350°F (175°C).
2. In a bowl, mix chocolate cookie crumbs, melted butter, and sugar until well combined.
3. Press the mixture into the bottom and up the sides of a tart pan.
4. Bake the crust for about 10 minutes, then let it cool completely.

For the Filling:
1. In a saucepan, heat the heavy cream until it just begins to simmer.

2. Remove from heat and add the chopped dark chocolate, butter, vanilla extract, black pepper, and a pinch of salt. Let it sit for a minute.

3. Stir the mixture until smooth and well combined.

4. Pour the chocolate filling into the cooled tart crust.

Savory Chocolate Ravioli

Visit our Savory Chocolate Ravioli, an exquisite dish that seamlessly marries the rich history of pasta with the modern allure of chocolate. Delve into the historical tapestry where cocoa, once revered by ancient Mesoamerican civilizations, transcends its sweet connotations to reveal deep, earthy undertones in savory applications. In this contemporary rendition, the pasta unfolds as a canvas, interwoven with the essence of cocoa, encapsulating a luxurious filling comprising ricotta, Parmesan, and an array of savory spices.

As your taste buds embark on this culinary odyssey, a symphony of flavors unfolds. Hints of cocoa gracefully entwine with the decadent herbed cheese filling, while a savory butter and sage sauce elevates the dish to unprecedented heights of indulgence.

Ingredients

For the Pasta Dough:
- 2 cups all-purpose flour
- 3 large eggs
- 1 tablespoon cocoa powder
- 1/2 teaspoon salt

For the Filling:
- 1 cup ricotta cheese
- 1/4 cup grated Parmesan cheese
- 2 tablespoons unsweetened cocoa powder
- 1 teaspoon dried oregano
- Salt and pepper to taste

For the Sauce:
- 1/2 cup unsalted butter
- 2 cloves garlic, minced
- 1 teaspoon dried sage
- Salt and black pepper to taste

For Garnish:
- Grated Parmesan cheese
- Chopped fresh parsley

Instructions

For Pasta Dough:
1. Blend flour, eggs, cocoa powder, and salt in a food processor until the dough forms.

2. Knead the dough on a floured surface until smooth. Wrap in plastic and let it rest for 30 minutes.

For Filling:
1. Mix ricotta, Parmesan, cocoa powder, dried oregano, salt, and pepper in a bowl.

Assembling:
1. Roll out pasta dough into thin sheets. Place spoonfuls of filling on half the sheets.

Savory Chocolate Ravioli (continued)

The palate becomes a playground, where the unexpected fusion of chocolate in a savory context beckons adventurous food enthusiasts. Savory Chocolate Ravioli stands as a testament to the art of gastronomy, inviting those who revel in pushing culinary boundaries.

This dish is an invitation to savor an innovative combination of familiar comfort and culinary ingenuity. Tailored for those who appreciate the interplay of sweet and savory, it promises a gastronomic experience that transcends the ordinary. Ideal for individuals who relish culinary exploration, this creation prompts a celebration where tradition and innovation dance in harmony on the plate. Allow the unexpected to unfold on your palate, and immerse yourself in the exquisite tapestry where tradition meets innovation, and every bite tells a story of culinary finesse.

2. Brush edges with water, top with another sheet, and press to seal. Ensure no air pockets.

3. Cut into individual ravioli using a cutter or knife.

For Cooking:
1. Boil salted water. Cook ravioli for 3-4 minutes until they float.

2. Drain ravioli and set aside.

For the Sauce:
1. Melt butter in a skillet. Add minced garlic and cook until fragrant.

2. Stir in dried sage, salt, and black pepper.

3. Add cooked ravioli to the skillet, gently tossing to coat with the sauce.

For Garnish:
1. Serve hot, garnished with grated Parmesan cheese and chopped fresh parsley.

Serving:
Pair your Savory Chocolate Ravioli with a glass of bold red wine, such as a Cabernet Sauvignon or Chianti, to complement the richness of the dish. Alternatively, a dry white wine like Pinot Grigio can provide a refreshing contrast.

For a complete meal, serve the ravioli with a side salad featuring fresh greens, cherry tomatoes, and a balsamic vinaigrette. The crispness of the salad will add a delightful texture and acidity to balance the savory chocolate flavors.

Pomegranate-Jalapeño Spicy Chocolate Guacamole

Explore the intriguing history and tantalizing tasting notes of Pomegranate-Jalapeño Spicy Chocolate Guacamole. Rooted in the ancient traditions of Mesoamerican cuisine, this guacamole variation combines the velvety richness of avocados with the bold flavors of cocoa, spices, and the piquancy of jalapeño. The addition of pomegranate arils introduces a sweet burst, echoing the historical appreciation for diverse and vibrant flavors.

This guacamole is a journey through time, embracing the legacy of cocoa in savory dishes. Tasting notes unveil a harmonious blend—a symphony of sweetness from pomegranate, the subtle heat of jalapeño, and the deep, earthy undertones of cocoa. A unique and memorable experience, this guacamole pays homage to ancient culinary roots while inviting the palate to revel in the fusion of sweet, spicy, and savory notes.

Ingredients

- 3 ripe avocados, mashed
- 1/2 cup diced red onion
- 1-2 cloves garlic, minced
- 1-2 tomatoes, diced
- 1/4 cup chopped fresh cilantro
- Juice of 1 lime
- 1 teaspoon ground cumin
- 1/2 teaspoon chili powder
- Salt and pepper to taste
- 2 tablespoons cocoa powder (unsweetened)
- 1-2 teaspoons hot sauce (adjust to taste)
- 1/2 cup pomegranate arils
- 1 jalapeño, finely chopped

Instructions

1. In a large mixing bowl, combine mashed avocados, diced red onion, minced garlic, diced tomatoes, chopped cilantro, lime juice, ground cumin, chili powder, cocoa powder, and hot sauce.

2. Season the mixture with salt and pepper to taste. Stir until well combined.

3. Gently fold in pomegranate arils and chopped jalapeño for sweetness and spice.

4. Adjust spiciness by adding more hot sauce if desired.

5. Taste and make any final seasoning adjustments.

6. Transfer the guacamole to a serving bowl.

7. Garnish with cilantro, pomegranate arils, and slices of jalapeño.

8. Serve immediately with tortilla chips or as a topping for tacos.

Chocolate Basil Bruschetta

As the concluding act in a multi-course meal, this Chocolate Basil Bruschetta serves as a palate-refreshing and subtly sweet finale. The crisp baguette, toasted to golden perfection, sets the stage for the surprising combination of fresh cherry tomatoes, basil, and finely grated dark chocolate. The play of savory and sweet notes provides a delightful transition from the preceding courses, leaving a lasting impression on the taste buds.

This dish is well-suited for those who appreciate culinary creativity and a departure from the ordinary. Its light and sophisticated profile make it an ideal choice to conclude a diverse meal, allowing guests to savor the nuanced flavors without overwhelming the palate. The unexpected addition of chocolate adds a touch of elegance, making this Chocolate Basil Bruschetta a memorable conclusion to a thoughtfully curated dining experience.

Ingredients

- Baguette slices
- 1 cup cherry tomatoes, diced
- 1/4 cup fresh basil leaves, chopped
- 1 tablespoon dark chocolate, finely grated
- 2 tablespoons extra-virgin olive oil
- Salt and black pepper to taste

Instructions

1. Slice the baguette into 1/2-inch thick pieces.

2. In a bowl, combine diced cherry tomatoes and chopped fresh basil. Grate dark chocolate finely and add it to the tomato and basil mix. Ensure it's a subtle addition, not overpowering the other flavors.

3. Drizzle extra-virgin olive oil over the mixture.

4. Season with salt and black pepper according to taste.

5. Toast the baguette slices until golden brown.

6. Spoon the chocolate-infused tomato and basil mixture onto each slice.

7. Arrange on a platter and serve immediately.

Pair this Chocolate Basil Bruschetta with a light and crisp white wine, such as Sauvignon Blanc or Pinot Grigio, to complement the fresh and savory notes of the tomatoes and basil. Alternatively, a sparkling wine or Prosecco can add a touch of effervescence to enhance the overall experience.

Pies, Cakes & Pastries

Savory Victorian Ginger Pudding with Cocoa

The Savory Victorian Ginger Pudding with Cocoa presents a visual mosaic of golden-brown layers and marbled textures. Aromas of ginger, thyme, and subtle cumin entwine, promising a flavorful journey. The moist and crumbly texture, influenced by breadcrumbs, is heightened by gooey cheddar if added. Upon tasting, a savory symphony unfolds—ginger imparts warmth, thyme and cumin contribute earthiness, and cocoa adds depth with a hint of smokiness. The fusion of savory and spicy notes is harmonious, leaving a gentle warmth and a subtle, pleasing bitterness.

This unexpected delight pairs excellently with roasted meats, offering a Victorian-inspired twist to the palate. The pudding promises a unique, flavorful experience, embracing the bold and creative spirit of Victorian culinary exploration.

Ingredients

- 1 cup all-purpose flour
- 1/2 cup breadcrumbs
- 2 teaspoons ground ginger
- 1 teaspoon dried thyme
- 1/2 teaspoon ground cumin
- 1/4 teaspoon ground black pepper
- 1/4 teaspoon salt
- 1/2 cup unsalted butter, melted
- 1/2 cup vegetable broth
- 1 teaspoon baking soda
- 1 large egg
- 2 tablespoons cocoa powder
- 1/2 cup finely grated cheddar cheese (optional)

Instructions

1. Preheat your oven to 350°F (175°C). Grease a pudding mold or individual ramekins.

2. In a mixing bowl, combine the flour, breadcrumbs, ground ginger, dried thyme, ground cumin, black pepper, and salt.

3. In a separate bowl, mix the melted butter and vegetable broth.

4. Dissolve the baking soda in a small amount of hot water, then add it to the butter and broth mixture.

5. Gradually add the wet ingredients to the dry ingredients, mixing until well combined.

6. Beat the egg in a small bowl, then fold it into the batter. Divide the batter in half. To one half, add the cocoa powder and mix until incorporated.

7. Layer the plain batter and cocoa batter in the prepared mold or ramekins. If desired, sprinkle finely grated cheddar cheese between the layers.

8. Bake for 25-30 minutes or until a toothpick inserted into the center comes out clean.

9. Allow the pudding to cool slightly before serving.

Brazilian Cocoa Coconut Fish Stew

This Brazilian Cocoa Coconut Fish Stew pays homage to the country's culinary tapestry. Inspired by the rich tradition of Brazilian cuisine, the stew artfully marries coconut and cocoa, reflecting the nation's diverse flavor profile. As the dish simmers, the coconut's sweet creaminess intertwines with the cocoa's subtle bitterness, creating a unique and harmonious blend. The tender fish, immersed in the velvety broth, absorbs these intricate flavors. The cocoa adds a nuanced depth, balancing the sweetness of coconut and elevating the overall umami experience.

With each spoonful, this stew is a delicious journey through Brazil's culinary history, celebrating the fusion of indigenous ingredients and global influences that define the nation's gastronomic identity.

Ingredients

- 1.5 lbs firm white fish fillets (such as cod or tilapia), cut into chunks
- 1 can (14 oz) coconut milk
- 1 cup fish or vegetable broth
- 1 onion, finely chopped
- 3 cloves garlic, minced
- 1 red bell pepper, diced
- 1 yellow bell pepper, diced
- 1 can (14 oz) diced tomatoes, undrained
- 2 tablespoons tomato paste
- 2 tablespoons unsweetened cocoa powder
- 1 tablespoon olive oil
- 1 tablespoon fresh cilantro, chopped
- 1 tablespoon lime juice
- 1 teaspoon ground cumin
- 1 teaspoon paprika
- Salt and pepper to taste
- Rice or crusty bread for serving

Instructions

1. Cut fish into chunks; season with salt and pepper; set aside.
2. Heat olive oil; sauté onions and garlic until fragrant.
3. Add diced bell peppers; sauté until slightly tender.
4. Sprinkle cocoa, add cumin and paprika; coat veggies.
5. Pour coconut milk and broth; ensure cocoa mixes well.
6. Add tomatoes with paste; simmer gently.
7. Let stew simmer for 10 mins; add seasoned fish.
8. Cook fish until opaque (5-7 mins).
9. Season with salt, pepper, lime juice, and cilantro.
10. Serve over rice or with crusty bread; garnish.

Argentinian Chimichurri Cocoa Steak

Steeped in Argentinian culinary heritage, the Chimichurri Cocoa Steak offers a modern twist on traditional flavors. Argentina's famed grilling culture meets the rich history of cocoa cultivation in this innovative dish. The cocoa infusion, inspired by the country's cultural diversity, adds a nuanced depth to the classic chimichurri blend.

As you savor each bite, the tender steak showcases the perfect harmony of savory notes from garlic, parsley, and red pepper, coupled with the subtle bitterness of cocoa. This culinary fusion reflects Argentina's culinary evolution, embracing global influences while staying true to its roots. The result is a unique and delightful experience that captures the essence of Argentina's gastronomic journey, where heritage and innovation come together on a plate.

Ingredients

- 2 lbs ribeye or sirloin steaks
- 1 cup fresh parsley, finely chopped
- 1/4 cup red wine vinegar
- 1/2 cup olive oil
- 4 cloves garlic, minced
- 1 tablespoon unsweetened cocoa powder
- 1 teaspoon dried oregano
- 1 teaspoon red pepper flakes (adjust to taste)
- Salt and black pepper to taste

Instructions

1. Combine parsley, garlic, vinegar, olive oil, cocoa, oregano, red pepper, salt, and pepper for marinade.

2. Coat steaks generously; let them marinate for 30 minutes.

3. Preheat grill or pan over medium-high heat.

4. Grill steaks to preferred doneness, about 4-5 minutes per side.

5. Allow steaks to rest briefly; slice against the grain.

6. Drizzle remaining marinade over sliced steaks; garnish with parsley.

7. Serve this unique Argentinian creation with your favorite sides.

Peruvian Chocolate *Aji Amarillo* Chicken

Rooted in the diverse culinary tapestry of Peru, the Peruvian Chocolate Aji Amarillo Chicken is a testament to the country's rich history of blending unique flavors. *Aji Amarillo* peppers, renowned for their vibrant heat, intertwine with bittersweet chocolate, creating a harmonious fusion that pays homage to Peru's indigenous ingredients and influences from Spanish, African, and Asian cuisines.

The dish unfolds with a depth of flavors, where the earthiness of cocoa enhances the robustness of the Aji Amarillo. Each succulent bite captures the essence of Peru's gastronomic evolution. Pair this distinctive dish with a light-bodied red wine or a citrus-infused Pisco Sour for a perfect balance. The Peruvian Chocolate *Aji Amarillo* Chicken offers a tantalizing experience, where history and innovation converge on the plate.

Ingredients

- 2 lbs chicken thighs, bone-in and skin-on
- 3 tablespoons Aji Amarillo paste
- 1/4 cup bittersweet chocolate, finely chopped
- 1 large red onion, finely chopped
- 4 cloves garlic, minced
- 1 cup chicken broth
- 1/2 cup unsweetened cocoa powder
- 2 tablespoons vegetable oil
- 1 teaspoon cumin
- Salt and black pepper to taste
- Fresh cilantro for garnish

Instructions

1. Season and sear chicken thighs in vegetable oil until golden brown.

2. Sauté chopped red onion and minced garlic in the same pan until softened.

3. Stir in Aji Amarillo paste; cook for a few minutes.

4. Add chopped chocolate and cocoa powder; stir until melted and blended.

5. Pour in chicken broth; simmer until the sauce thickens.

6. Return seared chicken to the pan; simmer until cooked through.

7. Garnish with fresh cilantro.

8. Serve the Peruvian Chocolate Aji Amarillo Chicken over rice or with crusty bread.

Colombian Chocolate Plantain Empanadas

Hailing from the heart of Colombian culinary tradition, the Chocolate Plantain Empanadas encapsulate the nation's love for the perfect balance of sweet and savory. This delectable treat draws inspiration from Colombia's abundance of ripe plantains and the rich cocoa heritage. Plantains, a staple in Colombian cuisine, are mashed and intertwined with bittersweet chocolate, creating a filling that harmonizes tradition with indulgence. As you savor each bite, the inherent sweetness of the plantains melds seamlessly with the decadent chocolate, delivering a delightful contrast encased in a crispy empanada shell. Pair these empanadas with a Colombian coffee, accentuating the chocolate notes, or opt for a scoop of vanilla ice cream for a luxurious dessert. The Chocolate Plantain Empanadas showcase Colombia's culinary finesse, offering a mouthwatering homage to the country's diverse and rich flavors.

Ingredients

- 2 ripe plantains, peeled and mashed
- 1 cup bittersweet chocolate, finely chopped
- 2 cups pre-made empanada dough (store-bought or homemade)
- 1/4 cup sugar (optional, depending on plantain sweetness)
- 1/2 teaspoon ground cinnamon
- Vegetable oil for frying
- Powdered sugar for dusting (optional)
- Dulce de leche for dipping (optional)

Instructions

1. Combine mashed plantains, chopped chocolate, sugar (optional), and ground cinnamon in a bowl.

2. Place a spoonful of the plantain-chocolate filling in the center of each empanada dough round.

3. Fold the dough over the filling, creating a half-moon shape; seal edges with a fork.

4. Heat vegetable oil in a pan; fry empanadas until golden brown on both sides.

5. Drain excess oil on paper towels.

6. Optional: Dust empanadas with powdered sugar.

7. Serve warm; optionally, dip in dulce de leche.

8. Enjoy the heavenly combination of chocolate and plantains in these Colombian Chocolate Plantain Empanadas.

Chilean Cocoa *Merquén* Corn on the Cob

Steeped in Chile's culinary heritage, the Chilean Cocoa *Merquén* Corn on the Cob is a nod to the nation's rich flavors and cultural influences. *Merquén*, a traditional Chilean spice blend, and cocoa, a product of Chile's growing artisanal chocolate scene, merge to create a savory and slightly spicy twist on classic grilled corn.

This dish pays homage to the country's indigenous *Mapuche* roots, showcasing their distinctive spice blend. Tasting notes reveal a harmonious dance between the smokiness of *Merquén* and the richness of cocoa, enhancing the natural sweetness of the corn. Pair this unique creation with a crisp Chilean Sauvignon Blanc or a refreshing pale ale to complement the smoky and spicy elements. The Chilean Cocoa *Merquén* Corn on the Cob offers a culinary journey through Chile's diverse flavors, blending tradition with innovation on every cob..

Ingredients

- 6 ears of fresh corn, husked
- 2 tablespoons unsweetened cocoa powder
- 1 tablespoon Merquén spice blend
- 2 tablespoons olive oil
- 1 teaspoon salt
- Fresh cilantro for garnish
- Lime wedges for serving

Instructions

1. Preheat your grill to medium-high heat.

2. In a bowl, mix cocoa powder, Merquén spice blend, olive oil, and salt.

3. Brush the ears of corn with the spice mixture, ensuring even coating.

4. Place seasoned corn on the grill; cook each side for 5-7 minutes until lightly charred.

5. Remove from the grill; garnish with fresh cilantro.

6. Serve with lime wedges on the side.

Moroccan Cocoa *Ras El Hanout* Beef and Chickpea Tagine

Rooted in Morocco's rich culinary history, the Moroccan Cocoa *Ras El Hanout* Beef and Chickpea Tagine offer a journey through the country's diverse flavors. *Ras El Hanout*, a blend of aromatic spices, intertwines with cocoa, creating a uniquely robust profile. This dish pays homage to Morocco's spice trade heritage and its influence from Berber and Arab cuisines.

As you savor each bite, the tender beef, chickpeas, and apricots are enveloped in a luxurious sauce that balances the warmth of *Ras El Hanout* with the depth of cocoa. Serve this tagine over couscous, allowing it to absorb the rich flavors. Pair it with a Moroccan mint tea for an authentic experience or a full-bodied red wine for a modern twist. The Moroccan Cocoa *Ras El Hanout* Beef and Chickpea Tagine encapsulate the essence of Moroccan culinary artistry.

Ingredients

- 1.5 lbs beef stew meat, cubed
1 can (15 oz) chickpeas, drained and rinsed
- 2 tablespoons *Ras El Hanout* spice blend
- 2 tablespoons unsweetened cocoa powder
- 1 large onion, chopped
- 3 cloves garlic, minced
- 1 cup dried apricots, halved
- 1 can (14 oz) diced tomatoes
- 2 cups beef broth
- Olive oil for cooking
- Salt and pepper to taste
- Fresh cilantro for garnish

Instructions

1. In a tagine or large pot, brown beef in olive oil. Add onions and garlic.

2. Sprinkle *Ras El Hanout* and cocoa powder over the beef. Stir to coat.

3. Add dried apricots, diced tomatoes, chickpeas, and beef broth.

4. Simmer on low heat for 2-3 hours until beef is tender.

5. Season with salt and pepper. Garnish with fresh cilantro before serving.

Simple Ras El Hanout Recipe:
1 teaspoon ground cumin; 1 teaspoon ground coriander; 1 teaspoon ground turmeric; 1 teaspoon ground ginger;1/2 teaspoon ground cinnamon; 2 teaspoon ground allspice; 1/2 teaspoon ground cloves; 1/2 teaspoon ground nutmeg; 1/2 teaspoon ground cardamom; 1 tablespoon dried rose petals; 1/2 teaspoon paprika; 1/2 teaspoon cayenne pepper (adjust to taste); Salt and black pepper to taste

Chile-inspired Grilled Spicy Sweet Potato

Dive into a culinary voyage with Chile-inspired Grilled Spicy Sweet Potatoes, a melange of bold flavors echoing Chilean heritage. This dish artfully combines the heat of chili powder, earthy cumin, and smoky paprika, creating a symphony on the taste buds. Sliced sweet potatoes, bathed in this flavorful Chilean spice blend, are masterfully grilled, offering a delightful balance of spiciness and natural sweetness.

Beyond a mere dish, it encapsulates the rich history of South American cuisine, where indigenous flavors meet contemporary grilling techniques. As you relish each bite, you embark on a cultural exploration, transcending borders and indulging in a culinary narrative that pays homage to Chile's diverse culinary tapestry, making this Grilled Spicy Sweet Potato an exquisite chapter in the ever-evolving story of global flavors.

Ingredients

- 2 large sweet potatoes, peeled and sliced into rounds
- 2 tablespoons olive oil
- 1 teaspoon chili powder
- 1/2 teaspoon ground cumin
- 1/2 teaspoon smoked paprika
- Salt and pepper to taste
- Fresh cilantro, chopped (for garnish)
- Lime wedges (for serving)

Instructions

1. Preheat your grill to medium-high heat.

2. In a bowl, mix together olive oil, chili powder, ground cumin, smoked paprika, salt, and pepper.

3. Brush the sweet potato rounds with the spice mixture, ensuring they are evenly coated on both sides.

4. Place the sweet potato rounds on the preheated grill. Grill for about 4-6 minutes per side or until the sweet potatoes are tender and have grill marks.

5. Remove the sweet potatoes from the grill and place them on a serving platter.

6. Garnish with fresh chopped cilantro and serve with lime wedges on the side.

Egyptian Cocoa Dukkah Spiced Chickpeas

With roots in Egyptian cuisine, *Dukkah* spice blend, a fragrant mix of nuts and seeds, adds depth to Quick Cocoa *Dukkah* Chickpeas. This fusion of cocoa and *Dukkah* brings a modern twist, marrying rich chocolate notes with the warm, earthy blend. Historically, *Dukkah* was a staple in North African diets, celebrated for its versatility. In this contemporary rendition, chickpeas are transformed into a crunchy, addictive snack.

Tasting reveals a harmonious interplay—cocoa's sweetness counters *Dukkah's* savory crunch. Sprinkle on salads, soups, or enjoy as a standalone treat. Pair with a zesty white wine or an aromatic herbal tea to complement the nuanced flavors. Whether elevating a simple snack or enhancing a gourmet dish, Quick Cocoa *Dukkah* Chickpeas offer a journey through time, weaving tradition and innovation into a delightful culinary experience.

Ingredients

- 1 can (15 oz) chickpeas, drained and rinsed
- tablespoons olive oil
- 2 tablespoons unsweetened cocoa - powder
- 2 tablespoons *Dukkah* spice blend
- Salt and pepper to taste

Instructions

1. Preheat the oven to 400°F (200°C).

2. In a bowl, toss chickpeas with olive oil, cocoa powder, *Dukkah* spice blend, salt, and pepper.

3. Ensure the chickpeas are evenly coated with the spice mixture.

4. Spread the chickpeas on a baking sheet in a single layer.

5. Roast in the preheated oven for 20-25 minutes or until the chickpeas become crispy, stirring once halfway through.

6. Once roasted, let the chickpeas cool slightly.

Easy Dukkah Spice Blend:

- *1/2 cup hazelnuts, toasted and chopped*
- *1/4 cup sesame seeds, toasted*
- *2 tablespoons coriander seeds, toasted*
- *1 tablespoon cumin seeds, toasted*
- *1 tablespoon black peppercorns*
- *1 teaspoon fennel seeds*
- *1/2 teaspoon sea salt*

Toast hazelnuts, sesame seeds, coriander seeds, and cumin seeds in a dry pan over medium heat until fragrant. Grind spices and nuts and add salt to taste.

Algerian Chocolate Cumin-spiced Couscous

Rooted in Algerian culinary traditions, the Algerian Chocolate Cumin-Spiced Couscous is a delightful fusion of flavors that marries the richness of dark chocolate with the warm spice of cumin. Historically, couscous has been a staple in North African cuisine, celebrated for its versatility. This innovative twist adds a layer of complexity, transforming a common grain into a unique and indulgent dish.

The tasting experience unfolds with the velvety notes of melted chocolate complemented by the earthy warmth of cumin. The aromatic spice blend, accented by coriander and cinnamon, brings depth to the couscous, creating a harmonious balance. The addition of nuts and dried fruits contributes texture and sweetness. Perfect as a side dish or a distinctive dessert, this couscous variation pairs exceptionally well with Moroccan mint tea, enhancing the North African influence, or a glass of sweet red wine for a touch of sophistication.

Ingredients

- 1 cup couscous
- 2 ounces dark chocolate, melted
- 1/2 teaspoon ground cumin
- 1/2 teaspoon ground coriander
- 1/4 teaspoon ground cinnamon
- Dash of cayenne pepper
- 1/4 cup toasted almonds, chopped
- 1/4 cup pistachios, chopped
- 1/3 cup dried apricots, chopped

Instructions

1. Cook couscous according to package instructions. Fluff with a fork and set aside.

2. In a bowl, melt dark chocolate. Mix in a pinch of ground cumin until smooth. Gently fold the chocolate mixture into the cooked couscous.

3. In a small bowl, combine ground cumin, ground coriander, ground cinnamon, and a dash of cayenne pepper.

4. Sprinkle the spice blend over the chocolate-infused couscous. Toss gently to ensure an even distribution of spices.

5. Mix in chopped toasted almonds, pistachios, and dried apricots for texture and sweetness.

Traditional Sage and Marjoram Red Wine Chocolate Beef Stew

Embark on a culinary journey with Sage and Marjoram Red Wine Chocolate Beef Stew, a contemporary twist on a traditional UK meal. Rooted in medieval flavors, this dish pays homage to the rich history of British cuisine while introducing an unexpected fusion of dark chocolate, red wine, and aromatic herbs. The sage and marjoram create a symphony of earthy notes, harmonizing with the robust essence of red wine and the indulgent depth of dark chocolate.

The result is a savory, tender beef stew with a luxurious undertone. This innovative adaptation invites you to experience the intersection of tradition and modernity, enticing your taste buds with a delightful blend of flavors that elevate a classic UK dish to new heights. Discover the intrigue and satisfaction of Sage and Marjoram Red Wine Chocolate Beef Stew - a compelling reason to embrace culinary exploration.

Ingredients

- 2 pounds beef stew meat, cubed
- 2 tablespoons olive oil
- 1 large onion, diced
- 3 cloves garlic, minced
- 1 cup red wine
- 2 cups beef broth
- 1/4 cup tomato paste
- 1/4 cup dark chocolate, finely chopped
- 2 teaspoons dried sage
- 2 teaspoons dried marjoram
- Salt and black pepper, to taste
- Mashed potatoes, for serving (optional)

Slow Cooker Instructions

1. In a large skillet, heat olive oil over medium-high heat. Brown the beef cubes on all sides. Transfer the browned beef to the slow cooker.

2. In the same skillet, sauté diced onions and minced garlic until onions are translucent. Add red wine to deglaze, scraping any browned bits from the bottom.

3. Transfer the onion and wine mixture to the slow cooker with the browned beef.

4. Add beef broth, tomato paste, dark chocolate, sage, marjoram, salt, and black pepper to the slow cooker. Stir to combine.

5. Cover and cook on low for 6-8 hours or until the beef is tender.

Oven Method:

Brown beef, sauté onions, mix with wine, broth, herbs, chocolate. Simmer in 300°F oven 2.5 hrs. Serve over mashed potatoes.

Bourbon Molé Pulled Pork Tacos

Delve into a flavorful journey with Bourbon Molé Pulled Pork Tacos, a fusion of tradition and innovation. Inspired by the rich history of molé, a Mexican sauce blending spices and chocolate, this recipe introduces a unique twist by infusing bourbon into the mix. The slow-cooked pork, bathed in a velvety blend of cocoa, ancho chilies, and aromatic spices, embodies a marriage of smoky sweetness and depth. The result is a succulent, bourbon-kissed pulled pork, perfect for assembling into tacos.

This creation pays homage to the centuries-old molé tradition while offering a contemporary allure. Venture into this culinary exploration to savor the harmonious dance of flavors, making Bourbon Molé Pulled Pork Tacos a compelling reason to reimagine and relish a beloved culinary tradition with a delightful chocolate-infused twist.

Ingredients

- 3 lbs pork shoulder, trimmed
- 1 cup bourbon
- 1 cup chicken broth
- 1 cup crushed tomatoes
- 3 dried ancho chilies, seeded
- 3 cloves garlic, minced
- 1 onion, chopped
- 1/4 cup unsweetened cocoa powder
- 2 tsp ground cumin
- 1 tsp smoked paprika
- 1/2 tsp cinnamon
- Salt and black pepper, to taste
- Corn tortillas, for serving
- Toppings: Shredded cabbage, sliced radishes, cilantro, lime wedges

Instructions

1. Place pork shoulder in the slow cooker.
2. In a blender, combine bourbon, chicken broth, crushed tomatoes, ancho chilies, garlic, onion, cocoa powder, cumin, paprika, cinnamon, salt, and pepper. Blend until smooth.

3. Pour the bourbon molé sauce over the pork.

4. Cook on low for 8 hours or until pork is tender and easily shreds.

5. Shred the pork using two forks and mix it with the sauce.

6. Serve the Bourbon Molé Pulled Pork in corn tortillas with your favorite toppings.

Oven Method:

Mix ingredients, place in covered oven-safe pot. Bake at 275°F for 4-5 hours. Shred and enjoy in tacos.

Cognac, Dijon Mustard & Cocoa Braised Short Ribs

Our Cognac, Dijon Mustard & Cocoa Braised Short Ribs fuse tradition with innovation, embodying the soul of classic comfort elevated to culinary excellence. Rooted in the rich history of slow-cooked indulgence, this recipe marries succulent beef short ribs with the bold sophistication of Dijon mustard. The choice of unsweetened cocoa introduces depth, balancing savory and earthy tones. As these robust flavors meld in a slow braise, the aroma fills the kitchen with anticipation.

This dish transcends its traditional roots, showcasing the evolution of culinary artistry. The result is a tapestry of taste, where each tender bite tells a story of centuries past, yet whispers the innovation of today. Dijon Mustard Elegance short ribs invite you to savor the past while embracing the future, making every meal a timeless celebration.

Ingredients

- 3 lbs beef short ribs
- Salt and black pepper to taste
- 2 tablespoons olive oil
- 1 onion, finely chopped
- 3 cloves garlic, minced
- 1/4 cup cognac
- 2 tablespoons unsweetened cocoa powder
- 2 cups beef broth
- 2 tablespoons Dijon mustard
- 1 teaspoon dried oregano

Dijon's dual dance in Cognac Cocoa Short Ribs and Riced Asparagus is a nuanced play, bold in the ribs, zesty in the veg. It's a culinary symphony where repetition becomes art, weaving a harmonious duet that elevates the dining experience with playful sophistication.

Braising Instructions

1. Season and sear short ribs in olive oil; set aside.

2. Sauté onions and garlic until softened.

3. Deglaze with cognac, scraping browned bits.

4. Stir in cocoa powder, then add beef broth, Dijon mustard, and oregano.

5. Return short ribs, cover, and braise for 2-3 hours.

Oven Method:

Roast at 275°F for 4-6 hours.

Slow Cooker Option:

Slow cook on low for 6-8 hours. S

Riced Asparagus with Lemon-Dijon Vinaigrette-
A side dish for the Cognac Cocoa Braised Short Ribs

Grating asparagus into a rice-like texture brings a unique and captivating element to the dish, elevating it beyond traditional preparations. This method ensures a delicate, almost ethereal quality to the asparagus, creating a canvas that readily absorbs the zesty nuances of the Lemon-Dijon Vinaigrette. The fine texture allows for a harmonious pairing with the succulent Cherry-Infused Cognac Cocoa Braised Short Ribs. As each bite unfolds, the riced asparagus offers a refreshing crunch that contrasts brilliantly with the unctuous richness of the short ribs.

This innovative approach not only introduces a textural intrigue but also enhances the overall dining experience, making each component distinctly discernible while synergizing for a symphony of flavors on the palate. The riced asparagus serves as a vibrant counterpart, ensuring a memorable and sophisticated culinary journey.

Ingredients

- 1 bunch fresh asparagus
- 2 tablespoons olive oil
- 1 tablespoon fresh lemon juice
- 1 teaspoon Dijon mustard
- Salt and pepper to taste
- Optional: Fresh herbs (parsley, chives), chopped, for garnish

Instructions

1. Wash and trim the tough ends of fresh asparagus.

2. Use a microplane or the fine side of a box grater to grate the asparagus into rice-sized pieces.

3. In a pot of boiling, salted water, blanch the riced asparagus for 30 seconds to 1 minute.

4. Quickly transfer the blanched asparagus to a bowl of ice water to stop the cooking process, then drain.

5. In a small bowl, whisk together olive oil, fresh lemon juice, Dijon mustard, salt, and pepper to create the vinaigrette.

6. Drizzle the vinaigrette over the drained riced asparagus.

7. Gently toss to ensure the asparagus is evenly coated.

Optionally, garnish with chopped fresh herbs like parsley or chives.

8. Serve this riced asparagus alongside Cherry-Infused Cognac Cocoa Braised Short Ribs for a delightful contrast of flavors.

Bordeaux-Inspired Barley and Game Meat Stew

Indulge in the opulence of Bordeaux-Inspired Barley and Game Meat Stew, a culinary journey marrying tradition and innovation. Rooted in the rich traditions of French cuisine, this stew pays homage to the esteemed Bordeaux region, celebrated for its exquisite wines. The tender game meat, soaked in a reduction of Bordeaux red wine, creates a symphony of flavors enriched by shallots and Dijon mustard.

Innovatively, unsweetened cocoa adds a velvety depth, elevating the dish to new heights. This creation beckons those who appreciate the fusion of rustic and refined, making it ideal for gatherings where sophistication meets hearty comfort. Whether shared among friends or presented at a festive table, this stew invites a diverse audience to savor a piece of French culinary heritage with a contemporary twist, embodying the essence of Bordeaux in every flavorful bite.

Ingredients

- 2 lbs game meat (venison, elk or duck), cubed
- 2 tablespoons olive oil
- 1 large onion, finely chopped
- 2 carrots, diced
- 2 celery stalks, diced
- 3 cloves garlic, minced
- 1 cup Bordeaux red wine
- 2 tablespoons tomato paste
- 1 tablespoon Dijon mustard
- 1 cup pearl barley
- 4 cups beef or game broth
- 2 bay leaves
- 1 teaspoon dried thyme
- Salt and black pepper, to taste
- 2 tablespoons unsweetened cocoa powder
- Fresh parsley, chopped, for garnish

Instructions

1. In a large pot, heat olive oil over medium-high heat. Brown the cubed game meat. Remove and set aside.

2. In the same pot, sauté chopped onion, carrots, celery, and garlic until softened.

3. Pour in Bordeaux red wine, scraping the bottom to deglaze the pot. Stir in tomato paste and Dijon mustard.

4. Return the browned game meat to the pot. Add pearl barley, broth, bay leaves, thyme, salt, and black pepper. Stir well.

5. Bring the stew to a boil, then reduce heat to low, cover, and simmer for 1.5 to 2 hours or until the meat is tender.

6. In the last 30 minutes of cooking, stir in unsweetened cocoa powder.

7. Adjust seasoning if needed. Remove bay leaves before serving.

Oven Method:

Bake at 275°F for 3-4 hours.

Slow-Cooked Chocolate Red Wine Chicken Curry

This culinary innovation, appealing to adventurous palates, resonates with those seeking a unique blend of flavors.

The slow-cooked Chocolate Red Wine Chicken Curry blends tender chicken with the rich depth of red wine and cocoa. *Garam masala*, cumin, and coriander bring warmth, complemented by coconut milk's sweetness for a balanced and robust symphony on the palate.

Red wine's depth complements chocolate's richness, and curry spices contribute complexity, creating a harmonious fusion of flavors. Chocolate's innovative use elevates traditional recipes, enhancing savory notes with versatility, turning ordinary dishes into extraordinary culinary experiences. It captures tradition's essence while pushing the boundaries of gastronomic delight.

Ingredients

- 2 lbs (900g) chicken thighs, bone-in and skinless
- 1 cup red wine (choose a full-bodied red wine like Cabernet Sauvignon)
- 1 cup chicken broth
- 1 cup coconut milk
- 1/4 cup unsweetened cocoa powder
- 2 tablespoons tomato paste
- 1 large onion, finely chopped
- 4 cloves garlic, minced
- 1-inch ginger, grated
- 2 teaspoons garam masala
- 1 teaspoon ground coriander
- 1 teaspoon ground cumin
- 1 teaspoon turmeric
- 1 cinnamon stick
- 2 bay leaves
- Salt and pepper to taste
- 2 tablespoons cooking oil
- Fresh cilantro for garnish
- Cooked basmati rice for serving

Instructions

1. Marinate chicken thighs with salt, pepper, garam masala, ground coriander, ground cumin, and turmeric for 30 minutes. In a skillet, sear chicken until browned. Transfer to the slow cooker.

2. In the same skillet, sauté chopped onions, garlic, and ginger until golden. Stir in tomato paste and cocoa powder. Cook for 2 minutes.

3. Add the onion mixture to the slow cooker with chicken. Pour in red wine, chicken broth, and coconut milk. Add a cinnamon stick and bay leaves. Set the slow cooker to low and cook for 6-8 hours.

4. Adjust seasoning with salt and pepper, discard the cinnamon stick and bay leaves. Serve over cooked basmati rice. Garnish with fresh cilantro.

Oven Method:

Bake at 300°F for 2 hours.

Sous-Vide Brandied Cocoa Nibs

This unusual recipe draws inspiration from the rich history of cocoa and spirits, combining brandy-infused cocoa nibs for a distinctive culinary experience. Cocoa nibs are the essence of cocoa beans, crushed to reveal their pure, intense chocolate flavor. This culinary innovation harks back to traditional infusions, where flavors are meticulously coaxed to create something truly extraordinary.

The mingling of brandy and cocoa, showcased in diverse applications from truffles to steak crusts, pays homage to the artisanal craft of flavor pairing. Embark on a journey where history meets innovation, turning a seemingly odd coupling into a harmonious symphony of tastes, encapsulated in each brandy-kissed cocoa nib. Whether atop a dessert or enhancing a cocktail, this recipe invites you to explore the delightful boundaries of flavor.

Ingredients

- 1 cup roughly ground cocoa nibs
- 1/4 to 1/2 cup brandy

Instructions

1. Place the roughly ground cocoa nibs in a vacuum-sealed bag.

2. Pour the brandy into the vacuum-sealed bag with the ground cocoa nibs, ensuring they are well-coated.

3. Seal the bag using a vacuum sealer to remove air and prevent leaks.

4. Set up a sous vide water bath with a circulator and preheat it to a low temperature, around 120°F (49°C).

5. Submerge the sealed bag in the water bath and let it infuse for 2-4 hours.

6. After infusion, remove the bag, allowing it to cool before opening.

7. Strain the infused cocoa nibs, discarding any excess liquid.

8. Use the brandy-infused cocoa nibs in recipes like the Sous-Vide Brandied Cocoa Nibs & Cocoa Onion Compote on Strawberry Focaccia or as a unique topping for desserts.

9. Store any leftover infused nibs in an airtight container for future culinary adventures.

Other uses?

1. Brandy-Infused Cocoa Truffles
2. Decadent Chocolate Martini Garnish
3. Cocoa Nib-Crusted Steak
4. Gourmet Chocolate-Covered Strawberries
5. Chocolate and Brandy Fondue

Sous-Vide Brandied Cocoa Nibs & Cocoa Onion Compote on Strawberry Focaccia

Indulge in the symphony of flavors with Sous-Vide Brandied Cocoa Nibs & Cocoa Onion Compote on Strawberry Focaccia. The cocoa onion compote introduces a rich, savory depth, harmonizing with the brandied cocoa nibs' decadent notes. The sweetness of fresh strawberries atop soft focaccia creates a delightful contrast. Those who appreciate a balance between sweet and savory, coupled with the nuanced essence of cocoa and brandy, will relish this unique creation.

The infusion of brandied cocoa nibs infuses each bite with an elevated chocolatey allure. Ideal for adventurous palates seeking a gourmet experience, this recipe transcends the ordinary, making it a delectable treat for those who revel in the artistry of flavor pairing and crave a delightful departure from traditional sweet offerings.

For Cocoa Onion Compote:

Ingredients:

- 2 large red onions, thinly sliced
- 2 tablespoons olive oil
- 1/4 cup balsamic vinegar
- 1 shot of brandy-infused cocoa nibs
- Salt and pepper to taste

Instructions:

1. In a pan, heat olive oil over medium heat.

2. Add thinly sliced red onions and sauté until softened.

3. Deglaze with balsamic vinegar, stirring to incorporate flavors.

3. Stir in the shot of brandy-infused cocoa nibs for a rich cocoa essence, and season with salt and pepper to taste. Simmer until the mixture reaches a jam-like consistency. Let the cocoa onion compote cool before use.

For Strawberry Foccacia:

Ingredients:

- 1 pound fresh strawberries, hulled and sliced
- 1 batch prepared focaccia dough (homemade or store-bought)
- Olive oil for brushing
- 2 tablespoons honey for drizzling

Instructions:

1. Preheat the oven according to the focaccia dough instructions.

2. Roll out the focaccia dough onto a baking sheet.

3. Arrange sliced strawberries on top, pressing them into the dough.

4. Brush with olive oil and bake until the dough is golden and the strawberries are soft.

5. Drizzle honey over the warm focaccia, and, once cooled, spread the cocoa onion compote over the strawberry-topped focaccia.

6. Slice and serve this unique sweet and savory delight.

Spiced Cocoa and Whiskey Pulled Chicken

This innovative recipe transforms ordinary chicken into a symphony of flavors, slow-cooked to perfection. Begin by nestling succulent chicken breasts in the slow cooker. A harmonious blend of rich cocoa powder, the warmth of whiskey, and a medley of spices creates a tantalizing marinade. As the aroma fills your kitchen, anticipation builds. Set the slow cooker on a low setting, allowing the magical alchemy of tastes to unfold over 5-7 hours.

The result is an exquisite melding of spiced, tender chicken that effortlessly shreds with a fork. The slow-roasting process at a gentle 275°F enhances the infusion of flavors, ensuring a culinary masterpiece. Elevate your dining experience by serving this delectable creation over a bed of fluffy rice or nestled in warm tortillas. This Spiced Cocoa and Whiskey Pulled Chicken is not just a dish; it's a celebration of gastronomic innovation and slow-cooked perfection.

Ingredients

- 1.5 lbs chicken breasts
- 1 lb of chicken boneless, skinless chicken thighs
- 1 cup chicken broth
- 1/2 cup whiskey
- 1/4 cup cocoa powder
- 2 tsp smoked paprika
- 1 tsp cumin
- 1/2 tsp cinnamon
- Salt and pepper to taste

Instructions

1. Place chicken in the slow cooker.

2. Mix broth, whiskey, cocoa powder, paprika, cumin, and cinnamon. Pour over chicken.

3. Cook on low for 5-7 hours.

4. Shred chicken and mix with the sauce. Season with salt and pepper.

Oven Method:

Slow-roast at 275°F for 4 hours

Chocolate-Beer Braised Pork Belly

Chocolate-Beer Braised Pork Belly, an exquisite fusion of flavors and textures that will captivate your taste buds. Begin by immersing succulent cubes of pork belly in a luscious concoction of stout beer, soy sauce, brown sugar, tomato paste, and the crowning touch – rich dark chocolate. This decadent medley transforms the humble pork belly into a culinary masterpiece. Slow-cooking in the oven at a low 325°F for 2.5 to 3 hours allows the pork to soak up the essence of the beer and chocolate, achieving a sublime tenderness.

Elevate your dining experience by serving this delectable creation alongside creamy polenta or atop velvety mashed potatoes. Chocolate-Beer Braised Pork Belly is not just a dish; it's an epicurean journey that harmonizes the robust flavors of beer and chocolate with the richness of pork belly, creating a symphony of culinary delight.

Ingredients:

- 2 lbs pork belly, cubed
- 1 bottle stout beer
- 1/4 cup soy sauce
- 1/4 cup brown sugar
- 2 tbsp tomato paste
- 3 oz dark chocolate, chopped
- 1 onion, sliced
- 3 cloves garlic, minced

Instructions:

1. Brown pork belly cubes in a pan.

2. Transfer to slow cooker. Add beer, soy sauce, brown sugar, tomato paste, chocolate, onion, and garlic.

3. Cook on low for 6-8 hours.

4. Serve over creamy polenta or mashed potatoes.

Oven Method:

Preheat oven to 325°F (163°C). Braise pork belly in a covered Dutch oven for 2.5 to 3 hours until tender.

Rum Chocolate Jerk Chicken Stew

This innovative recipe transforms ordinary chicken into a symphony of flavors, slow-cooked to perfection. Begin by nestling succulent chicken breasts in the slow cooker. A harmonious blend of rich cocoa powder, the warmth of whiskey, and a medley of spices creates a tantalizing marinade. As the aroma fills your kitchen, anticipation builds. Set the slow cooker on a low setting, allowing the magical alchemy of tastes to unfold over 5-7 hours.

The result is an exquisite melding of spiced, tender chicken that effortlessly shreds with a fork. The slow-roasting process at a gentle 275°F enhances the infusion of flavors, ensuring a culinary masterpiece. Elevate your dining experience by serving this delectable creation over a bed of fluffy rice or nestled in warm tortillas. This Spiced Cocoa and Whiskey Pulled Chicken is not just a dish; it's a celebration of gastronomic innovation and slow-cooked perfection.

Ingredients

- 2 lbs chicken thighs, bone-in, skinless
- 1/4 cup dark rum
- 2 tbsp jerk seasoning
- 1/4 cup cocoa powder
- 1 onion, finely chopped
- 3 cloves garlic, minced
- 1 can (14 oz) diced tomatoes
- 1 cup chicken broth
- 1 sweet potato, peeled and diced
- 1 red bell pepper, chopped
- 1 cup black beans, drained and rinsed
- 2 tbsp olive oil
- Salt and pepper to taste
- Fresh cilantro for garnish

Instructions

1. In a bowl, mix the dark rum, jerk seasoning, and cocoa powder to create a marinade.

2. Place the chicken thighs in a resealable plastic bag and pour in the marinade. Seal the bag and let it marinate in the refrigerator for at least 2 hours or overnight.

3. Heat olive oil in a skillet over medium-high heat. Remove chicken from the marinade and brown on all sides. Transfer chicken to the slow cooker.

4. In the same skillet, sauté onions and garlic until softened. Add diced tomatoes with their juice and scrape up any browned bits from the bottom of the pan. Pour the mixture over the chicken in the slow cooker.

5. Add chicken broth, sweet potatoes, red bell pepper, and black beans to the slow cooker. Season with salt and pepper.

6. Cook on low for 6-8 hours or until the chicken is tender and cooked through.

Oven Method:

275°F (135°C) for 3-4 hours

Muscovado Cocoa Pork

Muscovado Cocoa Pork is a culinary fusion, blending influences from Southeast Asian and global flavors. Rooted in slow-cooking traditions, this dish marries tender pork chunks with the richness of muscovado sugar and the deep, chocolatey undertones of cocoa powder. The addition of coconut milk, soy sauce, and aromatic spices creates a symphony of sweet and savory notes.

Though not tied to a specific ethnicity, its Southeast Asian undertones, especially with coconut milk, add a tropical essence. Lovers of adventurous, globally inspired cuisine will appreciate the nuanced taste profile. The dish caters to those seeking a harmonious blend of sweet and savory, making it a delightful choice for anyone intrigued by innovative, cross-cultural culinary experiences. Muscovado Cocoa Pork embodies a celebration of diverse flavors, perfect for those who relish exploration within the realm of contemporary, fusion-inspired gastronomy.

Ingredients:

- 2 lbs pork shoulder, cut into chunks
- 1 cup coconut milk
- 1/2 cup muscovado sugar
- 1/4 cup cocoa powder
- 3 tbsp soy sauce
- 2 tbsp vinegar
- 3 cloves garlic, minced
- 1 onion, sliced
- 1 cinnamon stick
- 2 bay leaves
- Salt and pepper to taste
- Chopped green onions for garnish
- Cooked jasmine rice for serving

Instructions:

1. In a bowl, mix together coconut milk, muscovado sugar, cocoa powder, soy sauce, and vinegar to create the marinade.

2. Place the pork chunks in the slow cooker.

3. Pour the marinade over the pork. Add minced garlic, sliced onion, cinnamon stick, and bay leaves.

4. Season with salt and pepper to taste.

5. Cover and cook on low for 6-8 hours or until the pork is tender and easily shreds.

6. Before serving, discard the cinnamon stick and bay leaves.

7. Serve the Muscovado Cocoa Pork over jasmine rice, garnished with chopped green onions.

Oven Method:

275°F (135°C) for 3-4 hours

Cognac Cocoa Chicken Liver Terrine with Red Wine Berries

Savor culinary finesse with our versatile Cocoa Cognac Liver Terrine, enriched with red wine berries. Begin by sautéing chicken livers, cocooning them in a decadent blend of cocoa, cognac, and olive oil. Simmer mixed berries in red wine until tender, harmonizing with thyme for a vibrant melody. Intertwine the berry-wine symphony with blended liver, introducing the earthy crunch of pistachios.

This sophisticated dish offers both slow cooker and oven cooking options, catering to your culinary preference. The slow cooker method ensures a gentle infusion of flavors over 2-3 hours, while the oven method at 325°F for 2-2.5 hours delivers a tantalizing aroma. Once chilled, each slice unveils a mosaic of textures and tastes. Embrace the richness of liver and the decadence of nuanced flavors, perfect for those who appreciate culinary artistry.

Ingredients

- 1 lb chicken livers
- 1/4 cup cognac
- 2 tbsp cocoa powder
- 1/2 cup mixed berries (strawberries, red currants)
- 1/2 cup red wine
- 1/4 cup pistachios, chopped
- 1 tsp thyme leaves
- Salt and pepper to taste
- Olive oil for sautéing
- Parchment paper

Instructions

1. Sauté chicken livers in olive oil until browned. Sprinkle with cocoa powder, add cognac, and cook until livers are browned outside but slightly pink inside. Blend livers until smooth.

2. Simmer mixed berries with red wine until berries are soft. Add thyme leaves during the last few minutes.

3. Mix the berry-red wine mixture into the blended liver. Season with salt and pepper. Stir in chopped pistachios for texture.

4. Line a dish with parchment paper. Pour the mixture into the dish. Cover and refrigerate for at least 4 hours or overnight until set.

5. Uncover, slice, and serve chilled. Enjoy with bread or crackers.

Slow Cooker Method:

Sauté livers in cocoa-cognac blend. Blend with wine-berry mix. Add pistachios. Slow cook 2-3 hrs. Set in dish. Chill.

Oven Method:

Sauté livers in cocoa-cognac blend. Blend with wine-berry mix and pistachios. Bake in a covered dish at 325°F for 2-2.5 hrs. Chill, slice, and serve.

Zero-Alcohol Celebratory Chocolate Punch

Indulge in the luscious creation of Chocolate Coffee Float Punch. Melt dark or semi-sweet chocolate chips into a velvety blend of heavy cream and whole milk. Infuse sweetness with sweetened condensed milk, cocoa powder, and a touch of powdered sugar. A dash of vanilla extract, optional cinnamon, and a pinch of salt elevate the flavor profile.

Combine this rich chocolate elixir with chilled cold brew coffee and effervescent sparkling water. The final touch: a scoop of chocolate ice cream or sorbet, creating a decadent float. Serve over ice cubes, and garnish with chocolate shavings. This recipe harmonizes the boldness of chocolate, the depth of coffee, and the effervescence of sparkling water for a delightful, chilled concoction perfect for any occasion.

Ingredients:

- 1 cup chocolate chips (dark or semi-sweet)
- 1 cup heavy cream
- 1 cup whole milk
- 1/2 cup sweetened condensed milk
- 1/4 cup unsweetened cocoa powder
- 1/4 cup powdered sugar (adjust to taste)
- 1 teaspoon vanilla extract
- 1/4 teaspoon cinnamon (optional)
- Pinch of salt
- 2 cups cold brew coffee, chilled
- 2 cups sparkling water or club soda, chilled
- 1 cup chocolate ice cream or chocolate sorbet
- Ice cubes
- Chocolate shavings or grated chocolate for garnish

Instructions:

1. In a saucepan over medium heat, combine chocolate chips, heavy cream, and whole milk. Stir continuously until the chocolate is fully melted and the mixture is smooth.

2. Add sweetened condensed milk, cocoa powder, powdered sugar, vanilla extract, cinnamon (if using), and a pinch of salt. Continue to stir until well combined and heated through. Be careful not to let it boil.

3. Remove the chocolate mixture from heat and let it cool to room temperature. Once cooled, refrigerate for at least 2 hours or until chilled.

4. In a punch bowl, combine the chilled chocolate mixture with cold brew coffee and sparkling water. Stir well to combine.

5. Just before serving, add chocolate ice cream or chocolate sorbet to the punch bowl. Give it a gentle stir.

6. Add ice cubes to the punch bowl to keep it chilled.

Cocoa Vinegar

This sophisticated Velvet Truffle Cocoa Vinegar infusion presents an intricate blend of rich flavors. Combining red wine vinegar, cocoa powder, dark chocolate, honey, and an array of spices, it undergoes a meticulous process, simmering to perfection. The addition of balsamic vinegar elevates its complexity, while a touch of dried cherries or cranberries adds a delightful fruity nuance. A unique innovation lies in the optional aging period, allowing the infusion to mature and intensify, unveiling layers of depth. The resulting elixir, stored refrigerated, finds versatile application in dressings, marinades, desserts, and cocktails, imparting a luxurious touch to culinary creations. This creation builds upon the precedent of traditional cocoa vinegar, introducing an intricacy that caters to the discerning palate, a testament to the fusion of time-honored techniques and innovative culinary exploration. Embrace this concoction to elevate your gastronomic experience with its nuanced symphony of flavors.

Ingredients

- 1/2 cups high-quality red wine vinegar
- 1/2 cup high-quality cocoa powder
- 1/2 cup high-quality dark chocolate (70% cocoa), finely chopped
- 3 tablespoons raw honey or dark maple syrup
- 2 teaspoons pure vanilla extract
- 1/2 teaspoon smoked sea salt
- 1/4 teaspoon cinnamon
- 1/4 teaspoon cayenne pepper (adjust to taste for subtle heat)
- Zest of one orange
- Zest of one lemon
- 1 small piece of vanilla bean, split (optional)
- 3-4 whole black peppercorns
- 2-3 whole cloves
- 1 star anise
- 1 small cinnamon stick
- 1/4 cup dried cherries or cranberries
- 1/4 cup balsamic vinegar (for added complexity)

Instructions

1. Combine all ingredients in a bowl.

2. Gently heat the mixture over low heat, stirring until the chocolate is fully melted.

3. Simmer for 10-15 minutes, stirring occasionally.

4. Cool and strain into a bottle.

5. Age in a cool, dark place for 1-2 weeks.

6. Refrigerate.

7. Serve in dressings, marinades, desserts, or cocktails.

Classic Cocoa Elixir

Craft a super-simple Classic Cocoa Elixir by infusing a full bottle of vodka with cocoa nibs, split vanilla beans, and honey. Allow it to meld in a cool, dark space for a week, yielding a versatile infusion. Enjoy its rich chocolate undertones alone or elevate cocktails with a delightful cocoa essence.

As a quirky and unexpected variation, consider adding a small amount of black garlic to the Classic Cocoa Elixir-infused vodka. Black garlic, with its fermented and sweet umami flavor, can add a mysterious depth that complements the chocolate undertones. Use one or two cloves of black garlic, finely minced or crushed, and allow the infusion to incorporate this unusual element. Experimenting with black garlic introduces a unique twist, creating a fusion of sweet, savory, and chocolate notes that may surprise and delight your taste buds. Adjust the quantity based on your preference, ensuring that the black garlic enhances the overall complexity without overpowering the infusion.

Ingredients:

- 1 full 750ml bottle of vodka
- 1 1/2 cups cocoa nibs
- 2 vanilla beans, split
- 1/4 cup honey

Instructions:

1.. Ensure the cocoa nibs are of high quality, and split the vanilla beans lengthwise.

2. Open the vodka bottle and add the cocoa nibs, split vanilla beans, and honey directly into the bottle. You will have to remove some of the vodka to make room for the ingredients.

3. Reseal the vodka bottle tightly and shake it well to mix the ingredients. Ensure that the honey is well distributed.

4. Place the infused vodka bottle in a cool, dark place. Shake the bottle periodically to facilitate the infusion process.

5. Taste the infusion after about a week to check the flavor intensity. Continue infusing for a richer flavor if desired.

6. If desired, strain the infused vodka through a fine-mesh sieve or cheesecloth into a clean bottle, removing the solid ingredients.

7. Store the Classic Cocoa Elixir-infused vodka in a cool place. Enjoy it on its own or use it in various cocktails, adding a rich cocoa essence to your drinks.

Notes on Balancing a Traditional and Avant-Garde Dinner Party

---

1. Introduction: Crafting Culinary Harmony
Hosting a dinner party that seamlessly marries tradition and avant-garde flair is an art form. This introduction sets the stage for an immersive culinary journey, exploring the delicate balance needed for a successful event, from preparing guests for the experience to effective time management.

2. Preparing Guests for the Culinary Adventure
Before the party begins, create anticipation by communicating the evening's theme. Emphasize the blend of traditional and avant-garde dishes, sharing anecdotes about menu inspiration to build excitement among guests.

3. Balancing Act: Traditional vs. Avant-Garde
A. Cohesive Theme: Ensure a common thread ties traditional and avant-garde dishes, harmonizing diverse elements.
B. Progressive Revelation: Gradually introduce avant-garde elements, starting with familiar flavors and incorporating innovative twists, building curiosity throughout the evening.

4. Time Management: The Art of Efficiency
A. Pre-Planning: Develop a detailed timeline for preparation, cooking, and serving, identifying tasks for advance completion.

B. Delegate Wisely: Enlist support for smoother operations, allowing focus on intricate details and guest interaction.

C. Efficient Plating: Opt for dishes with components prepared in advance for stress-free execution during the event.

5. Courses vs. Buffet: Tailoring the Experience
A. Courses for Intimacy: Offer a multi-course seated dinner for an intimate experience, fostering conversation and a curated culinary journey.

B. Buffet Dynamics: Choose a buffet-style setup for larger gatherings, encouraging a casual, interactive atmosphere with diverse offerings.

6. The Art and Engineering of Service

A. Plate Presentation: Elevate the dining experience with visually striking plate aesthetics for avant-garde dishes.

B. Timed Sequencing: Maintain a well-paced flow between courses, allowing guests to savor each dish without feeling rushed.

C. Interactive Elements: Integrate live cooking stations or a dessert DIY bar for dynamic engagement in the culinary process.

7. Conclusion: Crafting Lasting Impressions

Hosting a dinner party blending tradition and avant-garde elements is a canvas for creative expression. Balancing the familiar with the unexpected requires thoughtful planning and execution. As you navigate this culinary journey, remember that the ultimate goal is to create an unforgettable experience where each bite tells a story and every guest feels a part of the gastronomic symphony. Cheers to hosting an exceptional dinner party that lingers in the memories of your guests!

§

Recipe Index by Category and Page

Blue Cheese and Fig Chocolate Risotto 50

Pumpkin Sage Chocolate Risotto 51

Lavender Honey Chocolate Risotto 52

CONTEMPORARY RUBS AND MARINADES AND SPREADS

Mexican Chocolate Spice Rub 53

Mayan Cocoa-Rub 54

Southwestern Chocolate Ancho Rub 55

Aztec-Inspired Cocoa Pork Rub 56

Barbacoa Chocolate Espresso Rub 57

Cajun Chocolate Blackened Fish Coating 58

Adobo Chocolate Chicken Rub 59

Easy Mole-Spiced Beef Rub 60

Sweet & Easy Chocolate Chipotle Dry Rub 61

Tajín Chocolate Fruit Coating 62

5 Chili Mocha Cocoa Rib Rub 63

Grapefruit Chocolate Chicken Rub for Caramelized Crust 64

Maple Bacon Chocolate Pork Rub 65

Sesame Chocolate Soy Marinade 66

Super Easy Honey Chipotle Chocolate Glaze 67

Cherry Cocoa Rub 68

European Balsamic Chocolate Herb Coating 69

Coconut Curry Chocolate Rub 70

Ancient Arab Cocoa Coffee Rub 71

Smoked Almond Chocolate Pork Coating 72

Herb-Infused Chocolate Balsamic Glaze 73

Hazelnut & Fig Chocolate Spread 74

Bitter Strawberry Chocolate Marmalade 75

Nutty Blue Cheese Chocolate Spread 76

Spiced Pomegranate Chocolate Sauce 77

Smoky Chocolate Dijon Mustard 78

Garlic Infused Caramelized Onion Chocolate Gravy 79

1880s Tomato Chocolate Ketchup 80

Spicy Chocolate BBQ Sauce 81

Sweet and Tangy Chocolate Chili Hot Sauce 82

Chocolate-Cranberry Chutney 83

Savory Chocolate Pesto 84

Chocolate Coffee Steak Sauce 85

Balsamic Chocolate Fig & Plum Jam 86

Chunky Chocolate Chipotle Salsa 87

Indonesian Chocolate Tamarind Sauce 88

Honey-Ginger Soy Chocolate Glaze 89

Matcha Chocolate Teriyaki Sauce 90

Honey Mustard Dark Chocolate Dipping Sauce 91

Chocolate Honey Mustard Marinade 92

Pear, Onion, Rosemary and Chocolate Marinade 93

PIES, CAKES & PASTRIES

Chocolate Tomato Jam Layer Cake 94-95

Peppercorn and Chocolate Panna Cotta 96

Long Pepper, Chocolate and Mace Parfait 97

Bitter Chocolate No-Bake Cheesecake 98

English Oak Barrel Brownie Cake 99

Ancient Grain Crackers with Pistachio and Bitter Chocolate Ganache 100-101

Cocoa Nib and Raspberry Fool with Bitter Chocolate Espuma 102-103

SOUTH AMERICAN-INSPIRED SAVORY CHOCOLATE RECIPES

NORTH AFRICAN-INSPIRED SAVORY CHOCOLATE RECIPES

SLOW COOKING WITH BOOZE

SPECIAL PROJECTS

Final Thoughts

In the expansive canvas of culinary history, numerous unnamed chefs have undertaken daring experiments, reshaping the global gastronomic landscape. Picture the audacious individual who first pried open an oyster—an unsung culinary pioneer, driven by curiosity and hailed as the hero of an undiscovered taste. These uncelebrated explorers, motivated by hunger and a passion for innovation, have indelibly influenced our plates and palates.

Consider the accidental revelation of rennet in a sheep's bladder—an innovation that revolutionized cheese-making. In the Peruvian highlands, nameless cultivators experimented with various potatoes, adapting them to different elevations. The enchantment of yogurt, born from the alchemy of bacteria and milk, likely stumbled upon by an unheralded chef in pursuit of something intriguing.

This book is a heartfelt homage and gratitude to these culinary trailblazers—anonymous heroes who, through centuries, dared to expand taste and technique boundaries. Their spirit and efforts, often propelled by necessity, have enriched our culinary heritage. We owe them gratitude for every unexpected flavor, innovative cooking technique, and staple ingredient in our kitchens.

As we delve into avant-garde and traditional chocolate dishes within these pages, let's not forget the countless hands that toiled over centuries, contributing to the vast mosaic of culinary knowledge. This book celebrates the collective wisdom gained from innumerable kitchen experiments—some driven by hunger, others by the innate human desire to create, innovate, and share.

Expressing gratitude to these unsung culinary explorers, we acknowledge the debt owed to those who shaped our food culture. Through this book, we pay homage to their spirit, recognizing that each bite savored is a testament to the legacy of those preceding us. Here's to the anonymous chefs worldwide—the true architects of our culinary journey.

Happy Food Adventures! -

www.ingramcontent.com/pod-product-compliance
Lightning Source LLC
Chambersburg PA
CBHW071150120626
46546CB00006B/2195